STALIN
Order through terror

A HISTORY OF THE SOVIET UNION 1917–1953
Volume two

STALIN

Order through terror

Hélène Carrère d'Encausse
translated by Valence Ionescu

WITHDRAWN

LONGMAN
London and New York

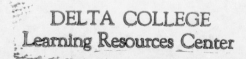

LONGMAN GROUP LIMITED
Longman House
Burnt Mill, Harlow, Essex, UK

Published in the United States of Am
by Longman Inc., New York

English translation
© Longman Group Limited 1981

French edition Staline, l'ordre par la terreur *first published 1979*
© Flammarion, Paris, 1979
English edition first published 1981
Second impression 1983

BRITISH LIBRARY CATALOGUING IN PUBLICATION DATA

Carrère d'Encausse, Hélène
  A history of the Soviet Union 1917–1953.
  Vol. 2: Stalin: order through terror
  1. Soviet Union – History – 1917 –
  I. Title
  947.084   DK265
  ISBN 0-582-29560-2

LIBRARY OF CONGRESS CATALOGING IN PUBLICATION DATA

Carrère d'Encausse, Hélène.
  Stalin, order through terror.

  (A History of the Soviet Union, 1917–1953;
v. 2)
  Translation of a modified version of pt. 2 of
the author's Union soviétique de Lénine à Staline,
originally published separately as: Staline.
  Bibliography: p.
  1. Soviet Union – History – 1925–1953.
2. Stalin, Joseph, 1879–1953. 3. Soviet Union –
History – 1917-. I. Title. II. Series:
Carrère d'Encausse, Hélène. Union soviétique
de Lénine à Staline. English; v. 2.

DK266.C283313 vol. 2 [DK267] 947.084 81-8132
ISBN 0-582-29560-2 (v. 2)   AACR2

Printed in Singapore by
The Print House Pte Ltd

CONTENTS

'The ideas of the ruling class are, in every age, the ruling ideas.'

KARL MARX (*Die Frühschriften*, ed. S. Landshut, Stuttgart, Kröner, 1953, p. 373).

'To maintain and transmit a value system, human beings are punched, bullied, sent to jail, thrown into concentration camps, cajoled, bribed, made into heroes, encouraged to read newspapers, stood up against a wall and shot, and sometimes even taught sociology.'

BARRINGTON MOORE Jr. (*Social Origins of Dictatorship and Democracy: Lord and Peasant in the Making of the Modern World*, Harmondsworth, 1969, p. 486).

INTRODUCTION

In 1917, the Revolution severed Russia from the whole of her past and with this unprecedented break she seemed to be set on the straight and predictable road to socialism. But it soon became clear that the path of history is far from predictable. The violence and radicalism of War Communism were followed in 1921 by the NEP. This was an enforced retreat from which men like Bukharin were to try to forge another road towards development and socialism, more in tune than was War Communism with society and its aspirations. In the years between the Revolution and the great turning-point of 1929, all options were still open to Russia, as the passionate debates of the 1920s showed. Should the change take place at the snail's pace which was natural to the peasants who formed the great majority in the country? Should it, on the contrary, be brought about at a demonic speed which would sweep that peasant society into an irresistible maelstrom? What had priority in the changing of societies: the structures or the states of mind? Should social structures be continually adapted to the states of mind? Or should, on the contrary, the states of mind, that is men and their aspirations, be forced to adapt themselves to the structures which were imposed upon them and which would shatter them? Until 1929, these questions remained unanswered and, because of this, the future of the USSR, the future of Soviet society, remained open. No historical fatality had as yet imposed a definitive choice, nor had the paths which the destiny of a people was to follow been determined.

But in 1929 the range of choice suddenly narrowed and the course which the history of the USSR was to follow was one from which there was to be no turning back. In deciding to apply, immediately and without any preparation, the economic programme of the Left, Stalin involved his country in a trial of strength and of violence which allowed for no alternative. Its history, from then on 'determined', can be understood better if the Stalinist plan in its entirety is understood. It was not only an economic choice that Stalin made in 1929. Over and above the economic change, he engaged his country in a total revolution, more radical even than that of 1917 in the diversity of its ends. This revolution, the Stalinist version of socialism, was made up of three aspects: the complete transformation of society through collectivisation and industrialisation; political revolution through the destruction of all the existing political structures and the atomisation of society; the creation of a new political society characterised by a new type of power – Stalinist power – and a new political culture. It was these changes, taken together as a whole and affecting society in its totality, which formed *Stalinism* and was Stalin's reaction to the old debate in Russia: how could this vast country be modernised? What did modernisation mean?

The Stalinist vision of the change, his choice of a total, radical and immediate change was marked, at first, by an absolute refusal to take the facts into account. The real state of the country, the aspirations of society, the means of realising the change which had been decided upon were all matters of complete indifference to Stalin. He believed tenaciously that political decision, thus man's will and power, were sufficient motivating forces in history. He pushed to the extreme the Leninist interpretation of Marxism. He made of the primacy of policy over the economy an iron law, which was to mark his every action, his every choice. He made of the voluntarism characteristic of Lenin the essential foundation of the changing of societies. But also, disciple of Lenin as he was, he knew that the will alone was powerless to move men; that to succeed in doing so, the will needs an organisation, an apparatus. Here again, Stalin took what he wanted from Lenin's ideas and interpreted them in his own way. In the Party, Lenin had created a privileged instrument through which he could enforce his political will. Stalin, in the same way, was to forge an instrument which would enable him to realise his planned transformation. But he did so ambiguously and this ambiguity was one of his additional strengths. Lenin's heir, eager to assert himself as such, Stalin constantly concealed himself behind the Communist Party, in order to emphasise what bound him to Lenin and what gave his power its legitimacy. But, in reality, he used the privileged instrument of his action, the repressive apparatus, to reduce the role of the Party to one of acting simply as a political and ideological support. It was this repressive apparatus which, under various names, was to be the instrument of Stalin's power and of his programme of change and was to enable him to secure his complete domination of the political system and society.

Chapter one

THE INSTRUMENTS OF STALINIST POWER

In the late 1920s having suffered reverse after reverse, Stalin's opponents suddenly became aware of the changes which were taking place in the power structure and of Stalin's growing authority over all the political apparatuses. Once they themselves had fallen victim to this change, they vehemently denounced the way the General Secretary was manipulating the Party in order to eliminate his opponents and to establish everywhere men who were his creatures. But these critics all had in common the fact that they either directly attacked Stalin's manœuvres, as did Bukharin, or tried to construct a theory of the deterioration in the Soviet ruling organs, as did Trotsky, and overlooked the essential, which was the shift which was taking place in the hierarchy of the Party apparatuses towards the security forces. Without ever proclaiming it, affirming on the contrary, the primacy of the Party, Stalin was, at the end of the 1920s and beginning of the 1930s, to change the Soviet political system drastically, by weakening the Party and by subjecting it to an instrument of the total power which alone was dominant, the police. The inadequacy of the Party to Stalin's transforming design partly explains this change.

FROM LENIN'S PARTY TO THAT OF STALIN

What was the Party at the time when it became the main instrument of Stalin's plans to structure the Soviet people in its forced advance towards socialism? In 1929 the Party was very different both from the organisation of heroic members assembled by Lenin and from the great Party which already existed in 1924. The change was both quantitative and qualitative.

The progress which had already been made is revealed by the figures. Lenin's 24,000 companions in 1917 had been joined since the Revolution by many members who in 1924 made up a Party of 472,000 members (350,000 full members and 122,000 candidate members). The Lenin recruitment nearly doubled these numbers which then rose to 801,804 members in 1925 (440,365 full members and 361,439 candidates). In the years that followed, the Party grew steadily and at the beginning of 1929, it already contained 1,535,362 members (1,090,508 full members and 444,854 candidates). Since Lenin's death, the Party had thus, more than trebled its membership and recruitment was, at that time, dominated by Stalin, whose authority over the apparatus through the secretariats was absolute.

In growing, the Party had changed in its essential characteristics. One of its permanent features remained, nevertheless, the preponderance of men. The Bolshevik Party had always contained a very small proportion of women and up to 1929 this situation had changed only very slowly. Women represented 13 per cent of the members of the Party as against 10 per cent in 1924. On the other hand, the Party had clearly grown younger and the political consequences of this rejuvenation were considerable. In 1927, 86 per cent of the members of the Party were under forty, 54 per cent under thirty. These figures reflect a young Party in which the place of the old Bolsheviks was constantly shrinking. It shrank in comparison with the whole – Lenin's companions were submerged in the flood of new recruits; it also shrank in terms of absolute value. Out of the 24,000 clandestine members in the Party of 1917, only half were to be found in the Party of 1922 and only 8,000 in 1929. Out of the 430,000 Party members in 1920, 225,000 still existed in 1922, 135,000 in 1927. All the others had disappeared, like the old Bolsheviks, during the various purges.

The conclusions which can be drawn from these figures are many and varied. First of all, the Party of 1929 had, in reality, not trebled its 1924 membership but had almost completely renewed itself, since it had at the same time expelled most of those who had been members in the 1920s. Thus, the Party of 1929 had been almost completely recruited during the 'Stalinist secretariat'. There were practically no old Bolsheviks in 1929 and barely 130,000 members who had experienced in the Party the epic of the Civil War. All the others had joined when debate in the Party had already been contained, when the spirit of discipline had already taken the place of the revolutionary initiative of the heroic years and of the criticism of the first years of the Leninist USSR. This, then, was a new Party, whose heroes, ideals and moral rules were no longer those of the Leninist Party.

At the cultural level also, the transformation of the Party was very important; the newcomers were of a very low intellectual calibre and were completely lacking in political experience. The main criterion on which they had been recruited by the secretaries was that of their blind obedience to the Party's authority, which became the new conception of the *spirit of the Party* (*Partiinost*).

This rejuvenation of the Party as a whole was all the more important in that it affected the rank and file, while at the top and within the apparatus the Old Guard remained. In 1929, 75 per cent of the secretaries of the large Party organisations had joined before the Revolution. Below them, in the primary organisations, however, the situation already reflected a transformation among the rank and file, since 65 per cent of the secretaries of these organisations had joined the Party after 1921. This state of affairs provides a partial explanation for the continual reverses suffered by the opposition, for its inability to base its resistance on the Party. The leaders of the opposition, whose only contacts were with the highest cadres in the Party, who, like them, had emerged from the first revolutionary generation, had not realised that, after 1924, two generations co-existed in the Party, their own and the one which had risen with Stalin's help. In 1929, all that was left for Stalin to do was to eliminate the higher cadres in order to achieve this change. This is why the purges of the years 1934–38 affected precisely those cadres.

Socially, also, the Party was changing. Lenin's Party had been a party of workers, a party rooted in the cities and the massive recruitment of the year 1917 had not changed the situation. Out of the 177,000 Party members at the time of the VIth Congress in August 1917, 40,000 came from Petrograd, 15,000 from Moscow, 20,000 from the industrial cities of the Urals, 15,000 from those of the Donbass. At that time, there were no communists in the countryside. After the Civil War, many peasants, who had joined the Party while they were serving in the Red Army, tried on their return to the villages to establish the base of rural communist organisations; however, then also, three communists out of five were to be found in the cities, although the urban population of the USSR represented only one-seventh of the entire population. Consequently, the preponderance of the urban Party became even more accentuated and in 1927, 73 per cent of the communists were concentrated in the towns and 27 per cent in the countryside. Until 1929, the Party was not only purely an urban Party but was still a Party concentrated in a few great cities (20 per cent of the entire Party was to be found in Moscow and Leningrad). But an urban party is often not a workers' party. The statistics of 1927 show that only 58 per cent of the Party were workers, out of which 36.8 per cent were manual workers. The rest were men with administrative functions in the various organisations. The same was true of the rural organisations in which only 11 per cent of the members actually worked on the land. As for the others, they were essentially bureaucrats, for the most part of urban origin. Within the Party, the growth of a whole stratum of State employees, whose status was very clearly defined could be seen to be developing.

An urban party, the Communist Party was also marked on the national level by the predominance of the Russian elements. In 1929, the USSR contained 47.8 per cent non-Russians, whose position in the Party was unrepresentative in spite of genuine efforts to improve it and the nationalities were often represented in a particularly unfair way as shown by Table 1.

This table shows the discrepancy existing between the over-represented nations in the Party, those of the Caucasus and of Byelorussia and those who were under-represented, primarily those of the Ukraine and Central Asia. Various explanations for these different situations are given. The favourable position of the Caucasians could be justified by the existence of the old and active social-democratic organisations, based on the workers in the oil installa-

Table 1. Representation of the nationalities in the Party

Nationalities	Percentage in the Party		Percentage in the population
	1922	1927	
Russians	72	65	52.9
Ukrainians	5.9	11.7	21.2
Byelorussians	1.5	3.2	3.2
Poles, Latvians and Balts	4.6	2.6	0.7
Minorities in the Russian Soviet Federated Socialist Republic	2	2.3	4.3
Caucasian peoples	3.4	3.6	2.5
Peoples from Central Asia	2.5	3.7	7
Others	8.1	7.9	8.2

tions and on a particularly dynamic intelligentsia. The case of Byelorussia is more mysterious. Conversely, the Ukraine, under-represented in the Party and very much more so in the ruling bodies (only 4% in 1926; 9% in 1929), seemed to reflect the general status of the predominantly agricultural regions, while the weakness of the Party in Central Asia reflected the difficulties in the way of a political transformation of societies in which the Muslim and national tradition was firmly rooted.

The situation in the Party was not exceptional, nor was that in the administration. At all levels of State power in the trades unions, and in the economic bodies, the Russians predominated, either because the national republics were short of administrative and technical cadres, or for political reasons or, again, because of a combination of the two. The habit, adopted during the Civil War of appointing the cadres from the centre in order to deal with the most urgent needs, had often been maintained and contributed towards the under-representation of the national cadres. The change in the ruling political body of the USSR in the course of the years was to be translated into many problems. The ruling bodies were continuously at grips with three concerns: they had to remedy the increasing 'deworkerisation' of the Party, to build more efficient structures in the countryside and especially among the non-Russian nations.

On 23 November 1928, *Pravda* announced that in two years the Party had to recruit 200,000 to 250,000 workers, to offset the opportunism which was developing among the communists. From then on, the broadening of the worker base of the Party was to be a theme brought up at every congress, even although it was widely acknowledged that the slogan of 1928 had not had any real effect. Nevertheless, in November 1928, the idea gained ground that the composition of the Party strengthened the deviationist currents and that it must be changed by a change in the membership and also by expulsions; this lay at the root of the purge of 1929.

Thus the Party, the essential means of the policy undertaken by Stalin in 1929 contained, in spite of the efforts of his apparatus, many elements of weakness, which were a poor preparation for the role which was to devolve upon it in the most difficult period of its history.

THE RISE OF THE REPRESSIVE APPARATUS

The repressive apparatus in post-revolutionary Russian was not

Stalin's creation. It appeared with the Revolution; it developed during the 1920s and Stalin in 1929 found an already very effective police system ready to hand. Conversely, the place of this apparatus in the Soviet political system, as well as its function, were specifically Stalinist innovations. In order to understand them, it is necessary to go back rapidly over the evolution of the police organisation in the period 1917–29. All revolutionaries have always denounced the role of the security services and asserted that once the Revolution had been made, it was up to the people themselves to watch over the security of the Revolution. However, when he took power, Lenin clearly decided that security was the concern of those with political responsibilities. This is why he created the Cheka (Extraordinary Commission to Fight the Counter-Revolution and Sabotage). At the time, Lenin justified this creation by the need to fight against internal enemies, in just the same way as the Red Army, which was to be forged the next year, was to fight external enemies. What needed to be done was to surmount the difficult stage in which the Soviet power was establishing itself and some Bolsheviks, like Zinovyev, proclaimed in 1918 that the Cheka was, by definition, extraordinary, and thus doomed to disappear at the same time as the counter-revolutionary dangers which it was supposed to stamp out, disappeared. In the period of internal tension, the Cheka was not, in Lenin's mind, an independent apparatus; it was the secular arm of the Party, completely subordinate to it and at its service. The man who was to direct it from its creation symbolised this subjection of the repressive apparatus to the political power. Felix Dzherzhinsky, its founder, was an old Bolshevik, a member of the Central Committee of the Party, to whom Lenin entrusted the setting up of a police force with undefined attributions and considerable powers, precisely through this lack of definition. The organisation grew rapidly and at the end of 1918 it already employed, according to Latsis, one of its first leaders, more than 30,000 members. While it was growing in numbers, the Cheka's duties and means of action were also taking shape. In January 1918 when Petrograd was suffering from famine, Lenin stated that the only remedy was the use of terror and the summary shooting of speculators.

From that time onwards, the Cheka used terror openly against anyone they suspected of being an actual or potential enemy. It arrested such people, beat them up or sent them to camps (which Lenin mentioned for the first time in August 1918 and which were made official by the decree of 5 September 1918) and which were to proliferate according to a process of which Alexander Solzhenitsyn has been the systematic and severe chronicler. This is not the place to describe again the history of the Gulag Archipelago, but it must be emphasised that as early as 1918 the repressive apparatus had already been created and the only limits to its powers was the political authority to which it was subordinate. Dzherzhinsky had been appointed as the man most suited to direct the institution because of his Party membership, his loyalty to the Party and its principles, as well as being fitted by temperament to do so. He was incorruptible and impervious to any appeal to sentiment when the interests of the Revolution or the Party were at stake, and he was to develop this formidable machine by which society was controlled without ever questioning its possible consequences. Roy Medvedev in his lucid study, *Stalinism*, tried to emphasise the great gulf between Lenin's action and that of Stalin in the terrible realm of the consolidation of a police apparatus by insisting that Lenin's objective was to strengthen his power; by insisting also on the means used, that is, on the choice of someone who would be responsible for the police and who was without personal ambition, completely devoted to the Party, and who because of this loyalty would guarantee the loyalty of the police to the Party and its objectives. No doubt this was true. But the fact remains that in 1918 Lenin accepted as the lesser evil that there should be an institution which was above the law, that it should be given vast powers and that violence and arbitrariness should be the privileged methods by which the political system was defended.

Lenin thought that the relations between the Party and the police had been established in a stable hierarchy and that consequently control over the police apparatus had also been guaranteed. But it took only a short time for it to become apparent that the edifice was extremely fragile and that there were dangers latent in the existence of a police machine which those who were engaged in Soviet politics might be tempted to use. In 1923, the changes in the name given to the police apparatus revealed both its institutionalisation and its permanent integration into the political life. The Extraordinary Commission (Cheka) was replaced by a Political Administration of the State (GPU) in 1922. The following year the GPU became the OGPU, or the Unified Political Administration of the State. From then on, the police apparatus wore a double aspect, that of an administration similar to the others attached to the Council of People's Commissars of the USSR, but also of an administration wielding excessive power.

From 1923 onwards, the field of action of the police apparatus extended to the Party and this was the decisive turning-point in relations between the two hierarchies. Dzherzhinsky had disagreed with Lenin's policy on the nationalities and in 1922 he had drawn closer to Stalin. It was not surprising then that in 1923, when the Party became the arena for an open struggle for Lenin's succession, that Dzherzhinsky was found on Stalin's side and that, at the same time, the police apparatus began to intervene in the struggle for the succession. When in October 1923 Dzherzhinsky presented a report to the Central Committee on the political situation, he asserted the right of the police organisation to exercise control over the Party members and the duty of the latter to co-operate with the OGPU in the struggle against the evil of factionalism. But from this angle, the Party lost its authority over the police and Dzherzhinsky claimed for his organisation the right to decide where truth and error in the Party lay. In practice from then on, the police were to become within the Party the tool of one group to be used against the others. From 1917, Dzherzhinsky's police had in the name of the Party hunted down its enemies outside its ranks. From then on nothing was to differentiate the Party's external enemies from those within it who were branded as enemies. It must be admitted that Dzherzhinsky did not as yet pursue to its logical conclusion the transformation of relations between the Party and the police and maintained a difference in measure between the way the two kinds of enemy were dealt with. Actual physical destruction until then had only been applied to those outside the Party. His successors crossed this threshold too. But the way the police institutions developed during the years when Lenin still dominated the USSR must be considered. In a few years, the police, set up as a fighting apparatus for the defence of the Revolution and also as an expedient, the provisional character of which alone justified, according to Lenin, its extensive powers and its arbitrariness, an apparatus in the service of the Party, became something quite different. It became a permanent apparatus of the State, legalised and institutionalised (it was mentioned in the Constitution) which extended its field of competence to the Party and intervened in its conflicts. From then on, illegal police action was given official recognition and admitted. And the Party's control over the police – the theoretical limitation of this illegality – tended to become the control by the police of the Party.

More than anyone else, Stalin realised the opportunities offered to him by this situation. He did his utmost to win Dzherzhinsky over to his side, because he knew that this incorruptible being was also a creature of strong passions who said of himself that he could only love or hate with his whole heart. To make certain of his support, Stalin helped him to realise an old ambition, that of assuming economic responsibilities. In 1924, after Lenin's death, when the time came for the positions of responsibility to be redistributed, Stalin ensured the appointment of Dzherzhinsky as head of the Supreme Council of the National Economy (VSNKH). This appointment was to have considerable consequences for the USSR. Dzherzhinsky was an ardent supporter of the NEP and of its gradualist approach to change. During the struggle for Lenin's succession which took place against the backcloth of the economic debate as to whether the NEP should be maintained or not, the head of the VSNKH supported the position of Stalin and Bukharin and as head of the secret police, threw all his weight on to their side against the opposition from the Left. The confusion between his police duties, those he exercised within the Party and his economic responsibilities enabled him to use the GPU machine for this purpose.

Although in the eyes of Stalin's adversaries, Dzherzhinsky was henceforth regarded as Stalin's man, the General Secretary himself knew that Dzherzhinsky could not be completely manipulated. His death during a stormy debate in the Central Committee in 1926 was to remove this last obstacle and enable Stalin to use the apparatus quite openly. From 1923, after the reorganisation of the GPU, Dzherzhinsky was surrounded by collaborators who were to succeed him. He had chosen two men who had taken part in the history of the Cheka from its beginnings, Menzhinsky and Yagoda, who became respectively vice-president and co-vice-president of the OGPU. On Dzherzhinsky's death, Menzhinsky succeeded him. In this ailing and unstable man who lacked both moral authority and the revolutionary past of Dzherzhinsky, Stalin found an accommodating ally. In 1927, Menzhinsky, in the struggle between the communists within the Party, resorted to methods of violence and espionage, unlikely to have been used by his predecessor. It was the extension to the Party of police methods hitherto reserved for the enemies of the people which enabled him to destroy the opposition of the Left and to isolate Trotsky. Outlawed and treated as though they were simply a band of conspirators, the Left was easily routed, as it was quite unprepared for this sudden irruption of police violence within the Party. Hitherto, the myth of a Party which, as an entity, was the source of authority had more or less survived. Menzhinsky clearly showed that the police recognised another type of authority, that of the Party apparatus, and thus of the General Secretary.

In 1929, when Stalin launched the USSR into total revolution, he already completely controlled the police apparatus. Menzhinsky, who was ill, was unable to withstand Stalin, even had he wanted to do so. At the end of the decade, moreover, his illness forced him to retire from the leadership of the OGPU where he was replaced by his closest collaborator, Yagoda, who had also entered the security services during Dzherzhinsky's period of office. In his book, *Stalinism*, Roy Medvedev dates the complete Stalinisation of the police from the time when Yagoda took over, and holds that, like Dzherzhinsky, Menzhinsky tried to maintain Party control over the police. This division between the 'good' Chekists, like Dzherzhinsky and Menzhinsky and the 'hard' ones who succeeded them is not supported by the facts. The evolution of the police apparatus, its intervention in the Party conflicts in favour of one group had begun very early. Besides, Yagoda, who, like his predecessors entered the Cheka when it was thought of as a counter-revolutionary weapon was no more capable than they of breaking all his links with the Party. Like Dzherzhinsky and Menzhinsky before him, Yagoda tried to handle carefully the team of the old Bolsheviks to which he belonged and was reluctant to treat Party members as though they were ordinary citizens. In spite of their great loyalty to Stalin, the heads of the police, so long as they belonged to the group which had been forged in the early days of Soviet power, tried to maintain the appearance of a unity of attitude of mind between the various apparatuses. This fear of cutting all links with the Party, of being no more than tools in the hands of the General Secretary alone revealed itself on two occasions.

In the early 1930s, Stalin clashed with a group led by Ryutin (a rightist who had rallied to the Stalinist theses) and who, seeing the defects in collectivisation tried to bring about a slowing down of the Stalinist programme and to remove Stalin from office. Although the GPU, under Yagoda's orders, tried to uncover and hunt down all the members of the group, he was less zealous when it came to destroying them physically. Because the evidence gathered by Yagoda was insufficient to justify the execution of Ryutin and his friends, the cases was sent to the Politburo who refused to sanction the physical liquidation of their own kind. Clearly, the moment there was any question of dealing with important Party members, Stalin was still unable to overcome Yagoda's reservations. The old rule enacted by Dzherzhinsky to preserve the life of the Party cadres was still observed. The same reservations appeared in 1934 when Stalin attacked the Party Old Guard. Yagoda flinched from the task of providing evidence against the Right. There are many documents which reveal Stalin's exasperation at the hesitations of the chief of police. Faced with these difficulties, Stalin proceeded in his usual way and reorganised the apparatus by changing the personnel. In 1934, the OGPU, radically transformed internally by the massive entry of new personnel, was dissolved and its attributions were transferred to the NKVD (People's Commissariat of Internal Affairs). Although Yagoda remained at the head – and he was to be harrassed by Stalin who accused him of being lukewarm in carrying out his task – the development of the NKVD was also marked by the rise within the apparatus of one of Stalin's protégés, Yezhov, who from 1934 controlled it. It was therefore not surprising that in September 1936 Stalin, by means simply of a telegram to the members of the Politburo, was able to force through the dismissal of Yagoda and his replacement by Yezhov. This imperative telegram gives the measure of Stalin's authority over the Party apparatuses and the police.

The choice of Yezhov throws light on Stalin's conception of a completely efficient police force. Unlike all his predecessors, Yezhov had not been a member of the old team of the Cheka, had taken no part in its gradual transformation and had not been marked by the discussions in the past on the links between the police and the Party. To this man, who owed his entire political career to Stalin, the police was a governmental instrument to which all men were equal and all were equally suspect, whether they were ordinary citizens or prestigious Bolsheviks. The privileged place of the Party in the Soviet political system which had long since been reduced to nothing or to almost nothing, but which had continued to exist in principle, vanished completely the moment Stalin established in positions of responsibility men who identified totally with him. The dividing line was not between 'good' and 'bad' chiefs of police; it lay in the past of these chiefs. From Dzherzhinsky to Yezhov, the ruthless character, the fanatical use of repression, of the men who dominated the Soviet police were the same; what differentiated them, however, was that Dzherzhinsky, Menzhinsky and Yagoda, who emerged from the ranks of Lenin's party, preserved, even although in an increasingly diluted form, some respect for the Party and for those who had founded it. Although they showed their merciless harshness and their unscrupulousness towards the population of the USSR at large, whenever it came to the Party they hesitated to treat it in the same way as the rest of society. In this resistance to his will – an ever-diminishing resistance – Stalin encountered some limits in his ability to act. But these limits affected the attitude of the police towards the communists only. Conversely, Stalin had been able very quickly to adapt the repressive apparatus to his plan to transform society by breaking it; and it is in this continual expansion of its attributions that the repressive Stalinist apparatus should be understood because here we touch on an essential characteristic of the Stalinist system.

At the outset, the Soviet police had fairly clearly defined attributions and its power was controlled by the Party. Allocated the task of hunting down the enemies of the Revolution, it acted as the Party's defensive weapon; it obeyed the Party leaders and depended on them. The extension of the institutions of the repressive system brought a rapid escalation of its powers. The use of terror, accepted by Lenin, as a necessity in order to traverse a difficult period, resulted in the police being given judicial attributions and, also through the constant growth in the number of suspects and internees, increased its own members. The exceptional powers of the Cheka were inscribed in its charter. In this document, which was not published at the time, it was stated that the Cheka should bring the 'saboteurs and counter-revolutionaries' before the revolutionary courts whose duty it was to try them, but at the same time its own explicit duty was to 'punish and liquidate' all activities which ran counter to the revolutionary interest. Furthermore, when on 14 January 1918 Lenin stated that speculators must be shot on the spot, he suggested summary executions when no court was available. From that moment the security services had the right to start legal proceedings and to take numerous decisions and the judicial body scarcely intervened. The proliferation of places of detention, of concentration camps which were the sole responsibility of the Cheka compelled it to increase its own apparatus, thus investing it with real power and autonomy.

But the most profound change in the status of the police, within the political system, took place in 1929 with the economic revolution. Until then, the arbitrary power of the Cheka had been directed towards the defence of the Revolution. After 1929, this arbitrary power took on an economic content. In fact, the OGPU played a decisive part in the collectivisation. It was the OGPU which helped to pin-point the 'kulaks' or those who were supposed to be kulaks; it was the OGPU which filled the camps with all the various 'enemies of the people' (peasants, saboteurs, priests, etc.). The camps were its sole responsibility. But, after 1929, the population of the Gulag Archipelago became a decisive element in the Soviet economic change. It formed in practice a cheap mobile working force, which was constantly renewable since, in order to fill its ranks, the OGPU had merely to make new arrests, to uncover new plots, the existence of which no one ever questioned. From that time, the repressive apparatus became also an economic one. Given its own economic means, the police was responsible, after 1929, for an enormous labour force which it had to supervise and structure. It also became the largest contractor in the USSR and its word in economic policy was decisive. The Party, divided and suspect, in which day after day the OGPU discovered new counter-revolutionary activities, was not large enough to take part in the economic revolution set in motion by Stalin. In his plan for radical transformation in which the technique needed to bring about the change was inadequate, the labour force became the main instrument of the change. Master of the labour force, the police apparatus ultimately decided the success or failure of the Stalinist undertaking. Never, in Russia nor probably in any other country, had the police such far-reaching functions. Never had it so great a degree of autonomy and power. The Stalinist system was built during these years on the police, not for its security but, and perhaps above all, for the realisation of its economic plans. The economist, Naum Jasny has clearly shown the part played by the labour force of the concentration camps in the realisation of Stalin's economic aims. Both a repressive and an economic apparatus, this double aspect explains how the police invaded everything in the USSR, how it left no room for any other apparatus, how it could penetrate everywhere and hold everything at its mercy including the Party. Between the police and Stalin a special relationship was established, because it was the main instrument by which his plan was carried out. To underestimate its economic role is to distort the entire Soviet political system during the decade of the 1930s.

The grounds for this phenomenal extension of the attributions of the repressive system which placed them in the centre of the political life of the USSR had been prepared by all the previous decisions. Dzherzhinsky, who filled the dual positions of head of the OGPU and of the Supreme Council of the National Economy, had built a bridge between the two sectors of public life which were usually kept separate. From that time, there had been a permanent overlapping of the two sectors. Under the NEP, the OGPU constantly intervened in the economy because one of its duties was to slow down the return to private enterprise, to see that the private traders did not become a rival political force in the USSR. After 1929, the trial of strength represented by collectivisation, the imbalances which resulted from it and the problems linked to an industrialisation with ambitious objectives for which nothing had been prepared, all implied that the role of the repressive structures would be determining. But the transition from this use of repression against society of which the police was the architect to the central economic function which it was to assume was not automatic. Everything was ripe for it; nothing made it inevitable. It was Stalin's conception of violent and radical change based on terror which led him to make of the repressive instrument the principal means of change. Stalin deliberately chose to found his whole project, his conception of modernisation on police violence, and this is why the two characteristics of Stalinism were social change by naked force and a political system in which the main apparatus was the police, but a police whose attributions and competences extended to domains which were not usually its responsibility.

The exceptional role played by the police apparatus in the 1930s also explains why the police and its values lay at the heart of the political culture which was then created in Soviet society. The contempt felt by all the revolutionaries for the repressive apparatuses and their methods was succeeded by respect for the tool which fought 'against the enemies of the people', the belief that this tool was particularly necessary in a society which was building socialism because it was in such a society, according to Stalin, that the enemies of the system were at their most dangerous. The privileges thus enjoyed by the members of the security services were a symbol of their usefulness in the Stalinist conception of power. However, in spite of the authority enjoyed by the police and of the domination which they exercised over all the other apparatuses, Stalin always maintained the fiction of a police which defended the interests of the Party and acted in its name. Even though the Party at that time tended to be reduced simply to its General Secretary.

Chapter two

THE SOCIAL AND ECONOMIC REVOLUTION

Stalin's political victory in 1928 was given concrete form by the adoption of the first Five-Year Plan which in a brief period was to change the material foundations and the structures of the Soviet economy. In fact, the planning adopted in 1928 had been in preparation since the beginning of the Soviet regime. From 1918 the directors of the Supreme Council of the National Economy planned its activities. During the NEP, the number of planning bodies was increased. In February 1920, the creation of the Goelro (State Electricity Company) had already made possible the beginning of a general plan of electrification. In February 1921, the Gosplan, the central organ of planning, prepared projects for a Five-Year Plan which would be definitively started in 1928. This plan was designed in the first place to develop the Soviet economy in a balanced and predictable way, to put an end to the distortions which for several years had weighed upon political life. This aim meant that there had to be a rigorous organisation of the needs and the means of which only the State, representing the general interest, could take charge. The 1928 Plan presupposed thus, above all, the passage of the whole productive apparatus into State control. The harmonious development of the Soviet economy was conceived as a means of economic and social progress; but from the first it was clear that one of the elements was to be privileged, that concerning the economy, the rapid progress of which was to enable social conditions to be modified. Here again, the choice of priorities, the progress of the economic base or the immediate progress of society meant a decision which was bound to be that of the State and strengthened the role which had devolved upon it.

These initial objectives determined quite naturally certain consequences of the Plan's application, above all its totalitarian character. The mobilisation of all the country's resources in the service of the Plan meant that the entire life of the USSR was integrated within it, that every activity was examined in the light of the planning needs. Another imperative and constraining aspect was added to the totalitarian one: the vastness of the aims and the clashes between particular and general interests naturally led to everything being subordinated to the Plan through the use of repression. Because the State alone was accountable for the general interests, because it alone disposed of the coercive means needed to subordinate individual wills to the general interest, because the Plan was the result of a political decision, the role of the State meant a concentration of means and a total centralisation; in practice, this meant a considerable increase in the bureaucratic apparatus in order to reconcile the excessive centralisation and the concrete problems of a vast and varied State.

The first Plan set itself two aims in 1928: to socialise the economy, and to develop heavy industry. In the agricultural field, the problem was not so much that of the level of production which had to be solved in the early days, but rather that of the entire restructuring of the peasant society which was to be brought about through collectivisation.

THE FORCIBLE COLLECTIVISATION

From the beginning of the Revolution, the poor peasants were called upon to farm collectively, but this first endeavour did not meet with success and the NEP strengthened the individualistic tendencies of the peasants. In 1928, barely 2 per cent of the peasants were members of the kolkhozes and an equally minute proportion of the State farms, created in 1919 (14,800 kolkhozes and 1,600 sovkhozes representing 2.7% of the cultivated area).

The collectivisation which was decided upon in 1928 was intended to solve three problems: the methods, the means and the political structure. As for the methods, the first Plan recognised only two forms of farming, the State farm which contained the state-employed peasants, whose produce was directly destined for the State, and the co-operative farms in which the peasants held in common their land, their livestock, their agricultural implements and their work. This type of collectivisation allowed for an autonomous peasant way of life, the peasants keeping their furniture, personal effects, some poultry, etc. The second problem was that of the material means put at the disposal of the peasants to enable them to measure the benefits of collectivisation. In 1928, the USSR possessed 27,000 tractors, whereas it needed more than 200,000. Stalin announced in 1930 that the production of agricultural material was growing rapidly and that in 1932 all needs would be met, but the fact remains that from the start the collective farms were short of every kind of mechanical equipment. The third problem was that of the political structure and this was linked to the composition of the Party. The transition to new structures depended upon the consent of the peasants, who had been prepared for the change and who were helped by competent cadres, able to organise the beginnings of collective life in a reasonable way.

It was these three problems, overlooked in 1928 and solved in haste and through improvised solutions which explain the confrontation which collectivisation brought about in the countryside. Conceived originally as a gradual operation – 20 per cent of the land was to be collectivised during the Five-Year Plan – and directed at first against the kulaks – 'We have passed from the liquidation of the class activities of the kulaks to the liquidation of the kulaks as a class', said Stalin – the character of collectivisation was changed by a decision of the Central Committee of January 1930 which substituted a maximum plan for the initial one. The collectivisation of agriculture was to be immediate and total. The resources necessary for this total change were to be supplied, by the terms of a decree of 1 February 1930, by the kulaks, all of whose possessions were to be confiscated and diverted into the reserves of the collective farms, while they themselves were deported. Thus, from the beginning of collectivisation, a series of decisions modified the rhythm and the methods accepted by the XVIth Conference and gave a new dimension to the peasant problem. In March 1930, five months after the beginning of collectivisation, 58 per cent of agriculture was collectivised. The peasants, uprooted from their farms, were hurled into agricultural structures in which nothing was ready to receive them and in which they were faced with insurmountable difficulties. Furthermore, this rapid collectivisation had taken the peasants by surprise. It was to be expected that all sorts of measures would be used against the kulaks, but the kulaks formed only 4 per cent of the population in the countryside; their resources were not unlimited and the confiscation of their goods was quite insufficient to make the collective farms viable. Furthermore, the definition of kulaks was vague and very quickly the authorities, who had to draw up the list of the kulaks and the goods which could be collectivised, tended to confuse fact and necessity and to treat as kulaks the middle peasants, to collectivise everything that the peasants possessed, their houses, their clothing, even as one reads in the Smolensk archives, their spectacles. Here we return to the problem of the integration of the peasantry. In order to draw up these lists, to force the peasants into collectivisation, on whom could the government rely? On the administrative authorities in the countryside, who were not usually of peasant origin, and who since 1927 had constantly clashed with the peasants and who remembered bitterly the pitchforks, even the guns, with which the collectors of cereals had been greeted?

In order to accelerate and to rationalise the movement, the Party set up in every village a special commission for collectivisation, composed of the secretary of the local organisation, the president of the committee of Soviets and the chief of the OGPU. To the peasants, and not only to the kulaks, these men represented the élites of the urban authority, men already divided from them by deep-seated hatreds. From the beginning, collectivisation assumed the aspect of a class war, in which the whole peasantry was in opposition to the authorities. The authorities met the violent peasant resistance with an equal violence which still further increased the bitterness. Many books published since 1956 in the USSR recount the drama and the horror of these months. The peasants slaughtered their livestock and gorged themselves to prevent their animals from falling into the hands of the Party. The kulaks or those who were described as kulaks ejected from their houses in the dead of night, in long despairing cohorts, half-naked in the Russian winter, left their dead strewn along the road to exile. In the collective farms, the dazed peasants refused to work. Whole villages were emptied of their inhabitants, and the stench of animal and human corpses hung like a pall over the whole countryside.

Very quickly, the authorities were forced to recognise the results of their voluntarism. Nearly half the livestock had been deliberately slaughtered, and the human losses were untold. On 2 March, *Pravda* published an article by Stalin entitled 'Dizzy with success' in which he denounced the results and put a stop for the time being to the increase of collectivisation. On 15 March, a decree authorised the peasants to decollectivise and those who were held responsible for all the excesses committed in the countryside were punished. Lastly, the measures of 'dekulakisation' (which admitted that the word kulak had been wrongly used) affected nearly 15 per cent of the peasants although only 4 per cent had been kulaks. The reaction of the peasants was immediate. The majority of them deserted the collective farms, the percentage of which fell to 21 per cent.

But this was only a brief lull and the XVIth Congress of the Party which met from 26 June to 13 July 1930 restated that the principle was correct. At the beginning of 1931, collectivisation started up again, more moderate in its methods, more gradual, but the movement was irreversible. In 1932, 61.5 per cent of the cultivated land was collectivised, (211,100 kolkhozes and 4,337 sovkhozes covering 88% of the cultivated area); by 1937 collectivisation was complete. By 1932, the socialisation of agriculture had been achieved, the private sector representing only an infinitesimal part. But the collectivisation marked the triumph of co-operative ownership over the complete State control of agriculture: the two sectors were to co-exist for a period which has not yet come to the end. In 1935, the IInd Congress of the Shock Kolkhozes adopted a statute of the type of the agricultural cartel and gave the kolkhoz co-operative its definitive form. The integration of the peasantry was achieved through the intermediary of the 'MTS' (Machine Tractor Stations) created in 1929, which were set up to modernise agriculture and its methods, but also and above all after the second Plan, to educate the peasantry politically by inculcating respect for socialist property and the discipline of work. In 1933, 'political sections' run by 25,000 Party members were grafted on to the MTS and accentuated their educational function.

THE COST OF CHANGE

Efforts undertaken in 1928 in the countryside had many social and economic consequences.

First of all, the structure of rural society was radically and definitively changed. The disappearance of individual farming and the collectivisation had been accompanied by an extraordinary displacement of people, due to the deportations and the regroupings. It was impossible to reconstitute the villages as they were before 1929 – a break had been made, of which the peasants were aware. The economic consequences were a result of the conditions of collectivisation. From 1929 to 1934, the herds of horses had been reduced by 55 per cent, the cattle by 40 per cent, the sheep by 66 per cent, and the pigs by 55 per cent. The production of cereals, except in 1930 when the 1913 level was slightly exceeded, fell disastrously; in 1932, it was 25 per cent lower than average. The

Stalin

dreaded famine, which had often been nipped in the bud since the NEP, reappeared. Rationing was reintroduced between 1931 and 1935.

But the most serious problem of collectivisation was the toll it took of human lives. No accurate assessment of the price paid by the Soviet peasants for Stalin's work as yet exists. As Basil Kerblay has so pertinently emphasised, the historian is better informed about 'the registered losses in Soviet livestock during that period than about the number of those exterminated for opposing the regime or as kulaks . . .'. Some indications, however, do give us an idea of the vast scope of the tragedy suffered by the Soviet peasants. Stalin himself once estimated the number of dead and deported at 10 million. Solzhenitsyn estimates that during collectivisation 5 million peasants at least were in the camps of Siberia and the far Arctic North. Another historian, Moshe Lewin, a specialist in the problems of the Russian peasantry, estimates that the deportation must have affected more than 10 million people, the majority of whom perished in the camps and roadworks. The famine of 1932–33 we know killed more than 1 million peasants. The enforced settlement was paid for by the death of 1 million people among the Kazakh people who before collectivisation numbered 4 million. These sinister figures appal the reader. No matter what sources are used, one ends up with millions of dead, with unimaginable sufferings, with a rural society decimated physically and doomed morally. Solzhenitsyn has stated that the collectivisation was above all an 'ethnic catastrophe'. This judgement which unequivocally condemns Stalin's policy towards the peasant is echoed in the research based on material in the archives of some Soviet historians, such as A. Barsov, who conclude that the total collectivisation of agriculture was 'an utter economic disaster'.

The disaster, the ethnic catastrophe were aggravated by the wholesale disorganisation of the Soviet economy which accompanied the execution of the first Five-Year Plan for which the peasants paid the price. In fact, after the introduction of rationing, the authorities tried, in order not to slow down the drive towards industrialisation to protect the industrial proletariat, from famine that is: the population of the cities which was needed for the construction which was being undertaken. Hundreds of thousands of peasants died of hunger during the years 1932 to 1933. Because the peasants were the source of food, they were ruthlessly dragooned. Those who stole grain were put to death and arrest and deportation were the usual punishment for producing less than was required or what was thought to be an insufficient amount or for any attempt to falsify the production. The effect of these measures was so unpopular, and led to such unbearable tension in the countryside that, as in 1930, the authorities beat a temporary retreat. A circular of May 1933 which long remained secret and was found in the Smolensk archives announced a slight rise in the price of cereals, a few concessions to the peasants, notably the right to a personal plot of land. More important, the circular set 'deportation quotas' for each village which were not to be exceeded. This suggests that this had indeed been the case. The structure of the countryside was changed throughout the first Plan but in the campaign the peasant, harrassed, starving and under duress, bitterly resented the violence done to him. The human failure of collectivisation was obvious.

INDUSTRIAL DEVELOPMENT

In industry, it was the goals of production which dominated and, ambitious as they were, they were nevertheless reached in many sectors. On the structural level, the existing independent enterprises were to disappear, their place being taken by the State enterprises placed under the authority of central managements. Two types of enterprise appeared at this time. The horizontal regroupings, production *trusts*, with wide powers, and vertical regroupings or industrial complexes. The complexes, grouping complementary trusts linked by the existence of a railway, encouraged regional development. This was the case with the Ural–Kuznetsk complex which linked the steel of the Urals with the coal of the Kuznetsk, or the Karaganda–Ural complex.

The aims of production were selective: heavy industry enjoyed an absolute priority and disposed of 80 per cent of the investments. Here problems appeared, first of all, that of the labour force, which was too small to reach the proposed objectives. The response was to use for the heavy work political prisoners whom work was supposed to re-educate. Kulaks torn from their land provided a handy and economic labour force. The inadequacy was also quantitative: qualified workers and technicians were in short supply and in spite of the efforts to speed up education, in spite of a period of indulgence towards the *specialists*, who were nevertheless denounced as rightists, this shortage held back the progress of the Soviet economy. The technical equipment was also inadequate and it was necessary to turn to foreign imports to fill the most urgent requirements which still further aggravated the problem of finance. The predicted investment for the first Plan was four times higher than that of the period 1918–28. Where were these resources which represented one-quarter of the national income to be found? The enterprises had to use their profits to finance some of the investments; the State, in turn, granted credits through the Bank of Industry and Trade. Finally, it was the nation as a whole which supplied the capital through its sacrifices.

In spite of these difficulties, the industrial balance-sheet was very different from the one presented by agriculture. Industrialisation had, at first, brought about a considerable sociological change in the USSR – the very rapid development of a working class which from 11 million in 1928 grew to over 38 million in 1933.

The economic achievements were spectacular; development of old centres such as the Urals, exploitation of new centres such as Magnitogorsk on the basis of lines of communication which linked the industrial regions together. Industries were created: chemicals, car manufacture, building of tractors. On the Dnieper, a dam and the most powerful hydroelectric power-station in Europe were the visible signs of the effort made, as was the Moscow underground, the pride from the beginning of the Stalinist regime. Overall, Soviet production increased by 250 per cent in the years of the first Plan, while the Western world was going through an unprecedented economic crisis. Nevertheless, these undeniable advances could not conceal the imbalances in production. The progress made affected some sectors of the production of technical equipment, mainly electricity and machines (in 1928 the USSR had to import 30% of its equipment in machines and only 13% in 1932). In other sectors, the results fell below the objectives – coal 80 per cent, steel, 60 per cent. Above all, consumer goods were completely sacrificed and the disappearance of the craftsmen (1% of the production in 1932) increased the shortages. In spite of the genuine progress (the finishing of Turksib, the building of the Stalin canal which linked Moscow to the White Sea), the distribution of produce and merchandise was inadequately assured. There were also increasing financial difficulties. In order to finance the Plan, the State had increased taxes, levied forced loans on wages before they were paid, taxed all profits and bought agricultural produce at very low prices in order to resell in the cities at a higher price. But these measures were not enough; inflation appeared, the fiduciary currency was multiplied by three, while the reserves of the Gosbank increased only two and a half times, prices continued to rise.

The successes and the imbalances of the Plan revealed the strengths and the limits of Stalinist voluntarism. Ill-prepared, often improvised, the leap forward of the Soviet economy had been partially achieved, thanks to countless sacrifices. Economists in the 1930s were critical of the irrationality of these great mutations. In 1931, the authorities staged a great trial in which were included the Menshevik economists who had criticised the theses, the historian Sukhanov and the old Marxist Riazanov, who from 1920 had denounced the two deviations of the regime, voluntarism and bureaucracy. Their condemnation was a sign that a new creed had triumphed: the foundation of Stalinist Marxism to which the economist Strumilin gave his support: political decision was paramount in a socialist State; economic and social conditions took second place.

However, the critics of the Left had emphasised something which was very important; this was the cost in human lives of the brutal transformation of Soviet society. The Left had accepted the idea that the peasantry should pay the price for the transformation, but in the first Five-Year Plan it was the whole society which had to pay the price of progress. It was true that the situation of the working class was better, in that it was not treated as the class enemy; it was not suspected of opposing the change. But, materially, the sacrifices imposed upon it were considerable. Wages rose very slowly and were subject to many pre-taxes, while the rise in prices reached 9 per cent per annum after 1928 as against 3 per cent between 1925 and 1928. After the progress of the NEP, the retreat was impressive. The fall in the standard of living in the years between 1929 and 1932 was estimated at nearly 40 per cent and the worker found himself almost in the same situation as he had been at the end of War Communism. The change was aggravated because it was accompanied by a growing inequality. Stalin explained his position on this point in 1931, by insisting on the link between the shortage of qualified personnel and the growing differentiation in salaries. In a period of shortages, how was it possible to pay skilled and unskilled workers in the same way? In applying these principles, an ordinance of September 1931 laid down eight categories of workers corresponding to very wide salary scales. The broadening of the salary range was accentuated by the gradual re-establishment in 1932 of the payment for piece-work instead of the hourly wage which to the workers had been one of the great gains of the Revolution, and by a complex system of productivity bonuses. The assessment of the norms which a worker could fulfil changed constantly and always tended to be raised.

A report under the auspices of Kuibyshev in 1935 gives some idea of the salary range. If the average wage was then 150 roubles per month, it went down to 80 roubles for women, from 100 to 120 for the labourers and rose to between 150 to 200 for qualified workers, 500 to 2,000 for shock workers. Although the engineers earned between 400 and 800, the high State employees reached salaries exceeding 5,000. This was a far cry from the figures supplied in 1928 by the trades unions which indicated that, whereas an average salary was from 80 to 90 roubles a month, the salaries of the highest state employees in Moscow reached 225. In 1933, 20 per cent of the urban workers received 40 per cent of the whole sum available for wages. Taking into account the considerable rise in food prices and the shortages at this time, one can see what the standard of living of the rank and file, condemned to an average wage, must have been. One understands also the need for a coercive system imposed upon a disenchanted and poverty-stricken working class, if the effort demanded of it was to be achieved. At the time, the supervision of the working class was carried out through the multiplication of repressive measures and the development of an apparatus of specialised supervision. From 1932, a series of documents formed a genuine Labour Code which continued to exist broadly until Stalin's death. An edict of 1932 laid down the penalties for unjustified absence (dismissal, withdrawal of ration cards, even eviction from one's lodgings when this was tied to the job). On 27 December 1932, the 'workbook' which chained the worker to the job was created; then the internal passport was added to these various restrictions on the freedom of the worker. Finally, in 1935 the trades unions were excluded from the discussion on the norms of work; the worker remained on his own, confronted by the management of the enterprise and by the State.

In order to impose this new situation on the working class, the authorities had to have at their disposal a large staff whose duty it was to supervise, but also to choose from among the working class those who composed its privileged elements, those who benefited from the inequality and who joined in this way the cohorts of the cadres, whose job it was to inspire and to reprimand at the same time. A workers' aristocracy was thus created – stakhanovites, heroes of labour – earning high wages and benefiting from many advantages even at the lowest level; rationing, for example, was not so severe for them. The Smolensk archives are very revealing in that they give whole lists of 'priority' categories in which, above the worker élite, one discovers a whole social stratum, the new Soviet intelligentsia – local cadres of the Party, of the Soviet, of the economy, specialists.

The growth of the GPU at this time was a response to the urgent problems of supervising a society in the process of wholesale change. In 1932, a great recruitment campaign was launched which admitted into the ranks anyone who would help it to carry out the many tasks assigned to it. During the period the GPU played an almost unfettered political, economic (because it was in charge of the deportees) and judicial role. Its task was particularly arduous in the cities in which the almost anarchic development posed daily problems of order and security. Industrialisation had brought with it the rapid growth of urban life which was not always controlled. The authorities had drawn off into the towns peasants needed for the enlargement of a working class which was still too small in numbers. This instigated movement was increased, before the establishment of the internal passport, by an exodus from the countryside born of despair, of the will to survive in conditions which it was hoped would be less harsh than those in the kolkhozes. Although the absorption of this population into industry did not cause excessive problems, its establishment in the cities which were often war-damaged, and in which the upkeep, even more than the building, of houses had made no progress since 1914, gave rise to housing problems which, added to the difficulties of provisioning, helped to embitter this still poorly integrated working class, and accelerated the growth of a police apparatus. In spite of all these difficulties, it was a transformed society which gradually emerged in chaos and shortages at the end of the first Five-Year Plan.

What Stalin eventually imposed upon his country was a 'great leap forward' in the economic field, destined, through the change of structures to create a new society. Did this vast project, with its terrifying consequences for human beings end at least in transformations worthy of the design and of the price which was paid? The economic limits and the imbalances engendered by the Stalinist options have been emphasised already. A Czech economist once drew the conclusion from the Soviet experience that 'great leaps forward are gymnastics, not economics'. Did the social change compensate for the poor economic gains? Without any shadow of doubt, one conclusion must be drawn about the USSR of the years 1934–35: the whole society had been thrown into an inexorable whirlpool, so that at the end of the ordeal no one remained where he had been some years earlier. Every individual had been displaced, uprooted from his environment, projected into a new world. The peasants had been thrown into kolkhozes or sovkhozes, camps, labour sites, cities. The village structure no longer existed in its original form. The workers had often been displaced geographically, sometimes promoted into the bureaucratic apparatuses which proliferated and constantly needed more employees. The urban milieu also changed because of the massive influx of new inhabitants and of the speeding up of industrialisation. Thrown, in their majority, into a world of suffering and of unimaginable efforts, sometimes promoted to tasks of supervision or of responsibility, all Soviet citizens found themselves in a new place in a totally changed universe. Did this human movement, unprecedented in its vastness and its rapidity, lead to the creation of a society of a genuinely new type?

For the superficial observer, the answer is undoubtedly that it did. In overturning Russian society, an overwhelmingly peasant one, it must be remembered that Stalin had wanted to extirpate it. He had wanted to hunt down first of all what to him symbolised the backwardness of his country, the peasant. To Stalin, the peasant was organised in a society closed within his own values, alien and opposed to the Soviet ideology. The peasant's visceral attachment to ownership of land, his diffuse religious feeling, his latent anarchism, all made him by definition 'the class enemy' which had to be uprooted and destroyed. In collectivisation, it was not only the kulaks against whom Stalin had a grudge. It was the *mujik* and his social culture which he outlawed. The well-ordered attack on the peasantry corresponded to an economic plan, but it was mainly inspired by contempt and hatred of the peasantry, by the determination to destroy it as a coherent society, organised around a living social culture. Through the chaos into which he hurled the peasantry, Stalin succeeded in uprooting him from his universe. But by treating him as an enemy, he failed to integrate him into the society which he claimed to be creating. Broken by the trials they had undergone and embittered, the peasants were for decades, to form an amorphous mass, a peasant nation which remained estranged from the Soviet rulers and their ideas. This separation between the peasant mass and the rest of society, between the peasant mass and the rulers, this alienation of the peasantry suggests the limitations of the work undertaken in the 1930s by Stalin. He had, it is true, collectivised and industrialised his country. But he had not succeeded in modernising it, because modernisation presupposes the integration of the whole society.

Chapter three
THE TERRORISTIC STATE

The economic and social transformation of the Soviet Union through industrialisation and collectivisation was accompanied by a no less important transformation of the political system. In general, what tends to be remembered from the years of the first Plans and from those which led up to the war are only the dramas and the disequilibrium and, at the political level, the continuous growth of a system of terror. However, the history of the USSR is more complex. During these years – the blackest the country had ever known – a new political system was gradually being built which served at the time as a support to the repressive system, but which also survived it. The USSR of the years 1933–38 was marked by a double advance, that of the terror and that of the State.

The Stalinist repressive system is widely known through Soviet documents (reports of trials) dating from the 1930s or later, like the analysis which Khrushchev made at the XXth Congress (1956). More than the facts, it is their logic which now faces the historian with a problem. Khrushchev, for his part, anxious not to jeopardise the whole political system, adopted a personalist explanation, pertinent no doubt, but definitely inadequate. For him, the Stalinist system was able to develop because Stalin was greedy for power and to establish his power, he eliminated first of all his adversaries, then seized by a mad lust for blood he struck at the whole Soviet people. The archives of the city of Smolensk give a far less orderly picture of this period; by enabling the reader to see who was purged, by what procedures, at what moment, by breaking out of the narrow circle of the leadership, to show the application of the purge at the regional level, these archives throw a fairly clear light on the evolution of the repressive system. They show that it was not a question of a system established once and for all, but of a system which, through an internal logic evolved, deepened and spread, after many fluctuations and retreats which reveal the resistance of the Party and perhaps also Stalin's hesitations.

The repressive system of the years 1933–38 developed in stages, some being more spectacular than others, always divided by lulls and measures of appeasement. The years can therefore be divided into five periods: the purges of 1933, a lull in 1934, a new wave of purges beginning at the end of 1934, a lull at the end of 1935 and the beginning of 1936, the period of the great trials of 1936–38.

THE PURGES OF 1933

The situation in the USSR on the eve of the purges in 1933 was ambiguous because the need to calm things down and the need for vigilance which led to the purges co-existed. After the tension of 1930, some desire to placate appeared, interrupted by harsh measures towards the peasants and the trial of the Mensheviks. But at the same time, within the Party, differences seemed to revive. In 1932, there were even two groups forming which defended, while remaining on the Right and on the Left, the same thesis, that of an economic relaxation (the maintenance of the essential measures of 1928 with some concessions to the private sector), in the hope that this would bring about political progress, a return to the democratic norms in the life of the Party.

It was probably the insistence on economic relaxation, a theme likely to attract the adherence of the masses, which disquieted the Party leaders who promptly labelled all such demands 'a rightist deviation', and forced those who made them to react. The result was the purge of 1933 which was restricted to the Party itself and which, consequently, took place relatively unnoticed by the country. On 28 April, a resolution of the Central Committee and of the Central Control Commission proclaimed the need to purge the Party of 'undesirable' elements and established six types of undesirables: 'the enemies of the people who sow discord in the Party'; 'hypocrites who conceal from the Party their desire to sabotage its policy'; 'those who violate Party discipline, that is who label as a fantasy the objectives assigned by the Party to the development of the USSR'; 'degenerates of bourgeois origin'; 'the ambitious and the careerists who have cut themselves off from the masses'; 'moral degenerates'.

This document resulted in the setting up throughout the whole of Soviet territory of purging commissions which were to operate from 1 June to midnight on 30 November 1933. In practice, it appeared that the main results of the purge (*Chistka*) were to eliminate from the Party the elements recruited at the beginning of the Plan and whose intellectual and ideological level was particularly low. It seems that about 10 per cent of the workers and as many peasants were eliminated and that the main charges could be distributed as follows: class enemies: 13 per cent; those guilty of playing a double game: 5 per cent; degenerates linked to the class enemies: 11 per cent; violators of Party discipline: 17 per cent; careerists: 8 per cent; morally corrupt elements: 18 per cent; passive elements: 27 per cent.

The general balance-sheet of the purge resulted in the expulsion of 22 per cent, but this figure does not coincide with the overall information concerning the Party members which decreased by 33 per cent at that time. It seems likely that the difference of 11 per cent represents voluntary resignations and takes into account the political situation which was developing in the USSR. It was in the Party that people felt that they were threatened rather than outside it, and they preferred to leave of their own volition, rather than to lay themselves open to expulsion.

At the same time, Stalin began a similar operation against the higher Party members. This time it was not a question of attacking new adversaries, but of discrediting even more those who had already been eliminated and whom he feared would take advantage of the fact that their own political programme was being put into effect to come near to positions of power once more. Under the pretext of the attack on the Party's economic policy which was led by Uglanov's former aide, Ryutin, who tried to associate the Left and the Right on a common platform, the Party expelled for a second time Zinovyev and Kamenev, who had been allowed to rejoin a few years earlier and who were accused of being sympathetic towards Ryutin's arguments. Other members previously excluded and then readmitted such as Smilga and Mrachkovsky were once again arrested and deported. Only those leaders who agreed once again to make a self-criticism escaped from detention or the camps, and once again public opinion helped to degrade those who had already admitted their faults, denied their friendships and promised to follow Stalin faithfully. Stalin emerged stronger from this new episode, which was still somewhat restrained in its dimensions, while the Old Guard of the Party sank even deeper into unpopularity. The arrests and the purge in the Party left public opinion relatively indifferent, because their application seemed to be restricted to the Party and because for the rest of the country there seemed to be some prospect of a calmer existence.

1934: THE YEAR OF UNANIMITY

There were many reasons for the relaxation which started at the end of 1933; in the first place there was the international situation which recommended prudence to the leaders of the USSR. Hitler had come to power on 30 January 1933 and this event brought about a profound change in the previous balance of power in Europe. A palpable threat loomed over the USSR which had to envisage its future in defensive terms. At the same time, on the plane of international communism, the policy drawn up at the VIth Congress had to be completely revised. The offensive tactics defined at that time which can be summed up in the slogan 'class against class' had helped, by dividing the German communists and the social democrats, to open Hitler's way to power. This course, which had been defended by Stalin in 1928, had led to one of the most dramatic failures of the Comintern and Trotsky, from his exile, was not content this time simply to denounce the mistakes of the past, but demanded the creation of a new International. Once again, Stalin, in order to justify his policy, needed the support of his colleagues. The leadership of the International and that of the Communist Party of the USSR had for years been too tightly interwoven for any condemnation of the International or for the creation of a new world revolutionary party, to the left of the first, not to be intolerable to the Soviet Communist Party. In order to isolate Trotsky from the Soviet opposition, to present his position as a purely personal one, a reconciliation was necessary; this took place at the XVIIth Party Congress which was held in January–February 1934. After the purges, the divisions and the anathemas of the past congresses, the XVIIth Congress presented an astonishing spectacle. The prisons had been opened, the Party had stepped up the number of readmissions and, with the exception of Trotsky, all the Bolshevik Old Guard was gathered at the Congress, Left and Right for once united around Stalin. By their presence, the opposition could thus find expression in a new climate in which insults had given way to applause. Of course, the opposition paid the price of this readmission by repeating its self-criticism; but the tone of the self-criticism had also changed; it was measured, serene and dignified. Stalin repeated what he had said in 1923: 'The Party is. united as never before.'

As always, Stalin dominated the Congress and the plaudits heaped on him were unstinted. However, this unusual gathering of men who had in the past been so divided could not be taken for a lasting reality. It was a sign, no doubt, of the Party's anxiety about the threatening external situation and the internal tensions which were able to weaken, temporarily at least, Stalin's position. It was also a sign of the search for a new equilibrium within the Party. The documents published at the conclusion of the Congress gave Stalin the title of 'Secretary' and not of 'General Secretary' which he had held since 1922. Considering how formal these proceedings were, this change cannot be attributed to an omission – it clearly represented a new allocation of duties and responsibilities.

The existence of a moderating faction within the leading organs of the Party was revealed by Khrushchev in 1956 and appeared in the documents. This faction seemed to defend the idea of economic and social relaxation and to rally those who were concerned by the growth in Stalin's personal power. Some had already, in the recent past, expressed their reservations about this power – Kalinin, Voroshilov, Rudzutak, Kirov. The Congress debated the objectives of the second Five-Year Plan and the final programme which was adopted proposed a development tax lower than the one which had been initially proposed. The needs of the people, the real capacities of men, were taken into account (light industries were to increase their production by 100%). This more realistic vision was again found in the measures adopted towards the peasants: many well-off peasants were amnestied; the peasant was allowed to cultivate a small plot, to sell his crops and to keep for himself a few animals (generally a cow, two calves, a pig, ten sheep, twenty bee-hives, some fowl and rabbits); the number of sovkhozes tended to decrease in comparison to the kolkhozes, in which a part of the land and livestock was exempt from collectivisation.

The less voluntarist and ideological character of the second Five-Year Plan showed very clearly that there had been an internal change, founded on a desire for relaxation which was favoured moreover by natural conditions. Good harvests at the end of 1934 made it possible to put an end to rationing. The noose seemed to slacken and the Soviet citizens could allow themselves to believe that with the end of the first Five-Year Plan the most difficult stage of the development of the USSR had also come to an end.

However, the XVIIth Congress produced not only signs of appeasement; on close examination despotic tendencies were visible. These were revealed especially by the rise in the governing bodies of men who were to play an important part in the years of terror: Yezhov, who became a full member of the Central Committee and entered the Orgburo and the Control Commission: Malenkov who was put in charge of the section of the cadres of the Secretariat: Poskrebyshev who was placed at the head of the special section of the Secretariat.

There were also changes within the institutions. The GPU was reorganised within the People's Commissariat of Internal Affairs (NKVD). The judiciary college, created during the Civil War, was removed from it and all matters falling within its competence were referred to the regular courts. The Supreme Procurator Vyshinsky was put in charge of its activities. In 1934, these measures were seen as improving the condition of the citizen, although in reality, they were very ambiguous. Did they reveal a desire to restrict the powers of the GPU? Or to make it more effective? Was the placing of the repressive apparatus under Vyshinsky's control an attempt to give him the means to supervise the legality of the institutions? Or to start to co-ordinate the instruments of the approaching purges? Both interpretations are possible. The measures of general appeasement seemed to favour the former explanation; hindsight suggests that, from 1934, a coherent repressive apparatus was being set up. Looking at the past history of the USSR, comparing the Congress of 1934 and that of 1923 in which Stalin had also stated that 'never had the Party been so unanimous', before engaging in the struggle in which he destroyed all his rivals one by one, one realises that there were similarities in the two situations. The same atmosphere of relaxation presided over both Congresses and in the shadows the same disquieting elements could be discerned: the setting up of a repressive apparatus, the rise of those who were to be the agents of the repression. It is very tempting to use this similarity to judge Stalin's real intentions and at the same time it is very difficult.

THE DEVELOPMENT OF THE TERROR: 1935

The period of appeasement came abruptly to an end on 1 December 1934 with the assassination of Serge Kirov, which remains to this day a mystery. The assassination was the prologue to a very dark period for the Party.

Kirov's assassination was the act of a young communist Nikolayev who was immediately arrested. He stated he had killed Kirov on his own initiative, without any instigators or accomplices, and was tried as such. But, from the beginning, there were doubts, which Khrushchev confirmed in 1956, when he suggested that Kirov could have been assassinated on Stalin's orders or, again, that Stalin could have known of the plot and that the GPU had turned a blind eye at his instigation, because the plot was in accordance with Stalin's own plans. In support of this hypothesis, Khrushchev presented an analysis of Kirov's position in relation to Stalin in 1934. Kirov, the docile collaborator of 1925 who at that time had crushed the Zinovyevist opposition in Leningrad, seems to have gradually emancipated himself in order to adopt in 1934 his own very individualistic attitudes. One of his Soviet biographers, Krasnikov, has stated that at that time Kirov was opposed to the repressive policy towards the peasants. This statement concurs with the opinion of Bukharin according to which Kirov in 1934 was the spokesman for the moderate trend, convinced that the success of the first Five-Year Plan should have enabled an end to be put to the terror and a return to legality in all spheres. It is known, moreover, that in 1934 there was a move to bring about Stalin's removal and it seems that the man put forward by the Party as his potential rival was Kirov. At the XVIIth Congress, Kirov, who had an exceptional position because he was supported by the Leningrad apparatus, received the loudest applause of all the delegates.

Although it cannot be proved that Kirov was assassinated deliberately, in spite of the many extraordinary details (Kirov's bodyguard was run over by a motor car just when he was about to give evidence at the inquest, many high officials in the Leningrad NKVD disappeared, etc.), it is clear that his death gave Stalin a pretext justifying the maintenance of the repressive system. The debate on the possibility of ending the exceptional measures was, from 1 December, completely superseded and, on the contrary, a simplified judicial system was established which, for four years, was to be the instrument of a generalised terror.

On the night of 1 December, a decision of the Central Executive Committee removed from those accused of plotting or carrying out terrorist crimes the normal rights of defence, ordered the Public Prosecutor's department to speed up the hearing of their case, suppressed the right to appeal for these crimes and ordered the immediate carrying out of the death sentence, the moment the verdict had been given.

On 4 December, *Pravda* announced the arrest of several high

State employees of the NKVD in Leningrad, accused of having 'at the very least lacked vigilance' and the condemnation and execution of 66 'Whites' whose activities and existence had been quite unknown. *Pravda* (6 and 8 December) was not very explicit about them, but emphasised that in view of the threats to the safety of the leaders, vigilance was essential. In the following week, this concern for vigilance was shown by the opening of three trials, this time of communists. On 28 and 29 December Nikolayev, who in spite of the fact that he had stated that he alone was guilty, was tried together with eleven co-accused. Convicted of having formed a 'terrorist centre in Leningrad' they were all condemned to death and executed at once.

The first trial of 1935 (15–18 January) saw the arraignment of many leading personalities, among them Zinovyev and Kamenev, who were accused of having set up a Muscovite centre with links with the 'terrorist centre in Leningrad' and which had instigated the activities of the latter, notably the murder of Kirov. Tried in camera, the accused once again acknowledged their faults and the court, finding them morally responsible, sentenced them to imprisonment: ten years for Zinovyev, five years for Kamenev and various sentences for the other co-accused. Some days later in Leningrad, the heads of the NKVD who had been arrested the day after Kirov's death, appeared in court together, charged in turn with complicity with the two terrorist centres which had already been denounced. Although they escaped prison sentences, for the time being, most of them were brought to trial again two years later and executed. At the same time as these spectacular trials were taking place and which were reported in the press, the NKVD increased its covert activity, throwing into prison old members of the Party like Georgy Safarov, and deporting many anonymous communists. Everywhere 'terrorist centres' were discovered.

However, even at this time, Stalin seemed to alternate between the increase of terror and conciliation. When he struck, he struck essentially at the old opposition of the Left and the 'Whites', while the Right seemed to be spared and Bukharin continued to edit *Isvestia* and took part in the drafting of the Constitution. Many old Bolsheviks, readmitted during the XVIIth Congress, kept their positions and those who were in disgrace were still given light sentences compared with the many death sentences given to their associates. There was no impression as yet that the repression was aimed at suppressing the Old Guard of the Party. However, the legal arrangements which extended the repressive system increased and the Party was to be subjected to a new purge.

These legal arrangements were extremely important; they transformed the terror within the Party into a generalised system of terror, threatening the whole country. By a decree of 30 March 1935 imprisonment was the penalty for anyone possessing fire-arms or weapons with blades. Soon it was to be dangerous to possess a kitchen knife. On 8 April the penalties of common law, including the death sentence were extended to children over twelve years old. On 9 June 1935 a new decree indicated the breadth of the purge which was being prepared by extending the death penalty, not only to spies and 'parasites', but to all those who 'were aware of such activities and projects relating to them'. This was a call for widespread denunciation and the establishment of the principle of collective responsibility which was, through the fear it inspired, to ruin for years social and family relations in the USSR.

At the same time, a new purge was begun by using the procedure of the exchange of cards. Already in 1933, at the end of the purge the Party had denounced the lack of order which existed in the granting of membership cards, which enabled dubious characters to infiltrate its ranks. In January 1935, a circular from the Central Committee enjoined all the organisations to unmask and expel the members of the Zinovyevist and Trotskyist opposition, by verifying their cards. The archives which can be consulted show that the zeal of the local organisations was very moderate and in June, and then in August, two new appeals were launched, far more threatening for the leaders who had not shown firmness and discernment (that is, who had not uncovered a sufficient number of suspects). Here the result was more positive since the balance of 10 December indicated that four-fifths of the members of the Party had been 'controlled' and that 9 per cent of those controlled had been expelled (7.5% of the expelled where the purge of 1935 had operated, more than 14% where there had been the purge two years previously). The Smolensk archives confirm these general indications showing that out of 4,000 members who were examined the Party pronounced 455 expulsions and kept 200 people on a special list until their case was clarified. Three reasons for expulsion appear: two-fifths of the expelled were described as 'alien and hostile elements', one-third as 'degenerate and suspect' and a small group had 'criminal antecedents'. On examination of the posts held by the expelled, it is clear that the objective of the purge was not the same as in 1933. The attention concentrated two years earlier on the rank and file members now shifted towards the men who held relatively important administrative positions. Above all, it was the State employees, the technicians and the teachers who were affected, but very seldom the permanent officials of the Party. Furthermore, the purge was politicised. The purge of 1933 had been aimed at excluding members of a very low level; here the political positions of those who were expelled were attacked, which meant that the consequences of the expulsions were far more tragic. Because those excluded were denounced as potential criminals, and because the principle of collective responsibility weighed upon the whole life of the USSR, their rejection by the Party for the most part prevented them from finding work and sometimes also affected their families. Rejected by a society which feared them, those excluded also frightened the Party which feared their reactions of despair. The archives show that this problem was widely discussed by the central and local organs of the Party which realised at the time that expulsion was possibly not enough to neutralise those whom it had 'unmasked as enemies'. Another interesting piece of information supplied by the archives, which reveals the moral evolution of the Party at the time concerns the high number of denunciations which made the purge easier. In Smolensk, 4,000 of those controlled were supported by 712 oral denunciations and 200 written ones.

The end of 1935 and the beginning of 1936 saw a new internal relaxation. Good harvests had enabled the progress of 1934 to be crowned by the suppression of all food rationing. Industrial production also improved because of this and the economic successes gave rise once again to the hope that the political tension itself might relax. This optimism, moderate as it was, was encouraged by the expectation of the publication of the new Constitution on which both Bukharin and Radek were working. It was possible to hope that the Constitution would lead to a degree of legality. But well before the promulgation of the Constitution of 1936, the *détente* came to an end, and the USSR was to plunge once again into the vicious circle of purges. At the end of 1935, this brutal break could not as yet be foreseen, and the citizens were encouraged to discuss their rights and their protection. The great jurist Pashukanis, who at that time edited the journal *Sovetskoy Gosudarstvo* (The Soviet State) became, at the conclusion of the drafting of the new Criminal Code, the apostle of the abolition of the death penalty and of a shortening of the terms of imprisonment. This code was never published because of the 'counter-revolutionary ideas' which it expressed, but the discussions which developed at the time helped to create the impression of a genuine change in political life.

However, although political life seemed to be becoming normal, the administrative purges within the Party were not yet finished. By the end of 1935 most of the members had been 'controlled' and it was possible to hope that the exclusion of all the suspected elements marked the end of the trials. On 14 January 1936 the Central Committee destroyed this hope by sending out an instruction to all the Party organisations concerning the issue of new cards. The directives clearly show that this was not a technical operation, but a new purge designed to exclude once again a new category of unsatisfactory communists, the 'passive elements'. This was a very disquieting expression, because although it was a simple matter to define categories such as 'alien to the Party because of social origin or social behaviour', how could the limits of passivity be laid down? What was activism in the tense atmosphere of 1936?

The vagueness of the directives, and fatigue too, explain the reluctance with which the organisations applied them. On the average only 2.3 per cent of the members and 1.2 per cent of the candidates were expelled by the Party during the operation. But the Party leadership considered that this was inadequate and on 19 July 1936 a secret circular of the Central Committee denounced the lukewarmness of the local organisations. 'In the present circumstances, the fundamental quality of every Bolshevik must be to know how to recognise an enemy of the Party, no matter how well disguised he may be'. Some months later, the organ of the Central Committee *Partiinoe Stroitelstvo* (2 January 1937) gave a more precise definition of a good communist, who alone was fit to remain within the ranks of the Party: 'Our Leninist-Stalinist Party demands again and again that every Party official and every communist should be able to identify and unmask, relentlessly and immediately the enemies of the people, the hypocrites and the Trotskyist-Zinovyevists, no matter under what disguise they conceal themselves.'

The task of the communists was thus to act as the vanguard in the hunt for the enemy of the people and not to assume this task was to reveal that one was an enemy of the people oneself. The effect of the June circular and the appeals of the Party describing it were immediate. Denunciations increased both within the Party and outside it, and the purges were extended. However, although up to this point it is possible to follow, within the Party at least, the stages and the logic of the purges, from the middle of 1936 it becomes impossible to disentangle the different elements of the terror as the process of the purge was speeded up, the grievances and the directives became intermingled and, above all, because the more or less anonymous purges were replaced by the great trials. From then onwards, all the minor and local affairs were tied into great charges which in Moscow resulted in spectacular trials, with the Party on one side and the main leaders of the opposition on the other. Every trial, every group seemed to be at the heart of a huge plot with ramifications extending to all regions of the USSR, to all echelons of the Party, to all the strata of society. For two years, the purges were no longer concerned with moral charges (passivity, hypocrisy, etc.) but with membership of a 'Zinovyevist' group, 'rightist' etc.; the *yezhovshchina*, or use of terror, was given a free hand.

THE GREAT TRIALS (1936–1938)

Up to 1936, the purges had spared the Old Guard of the Party, or at least its best-known leaders. In 1936 the Party, after so many purges and constant threats, seemed prepared to accept the immolation of its founders. Fear replaced every other feeling. The *yezhovshchina*, in three major trials, in a series of minor ones, trials in camera and summary executions without trial, was about to bring to fruition the work begun years before and to eliminate, physically this time, all the Old Guard, who had been many times discredited and expelled, but who had still survived.

The first of the great public trials began in August 1936 against the *terrorist counter-revolutionary Trotskyist-Zinovyevist bloc*. Among the sixteen accused grouped under this sonorous title were Zinovyev, Kamenev, Mrachkovsky, Yevdokimov, Bakayev, Ivan Smirnov, etc. In this relatively heterogeneous group of individuals some common elements could be discerned: most of them belonged to the Left; they were for the most part morally and physically exhausted by successive terms of imprisonment; they were largely discredited by their many former recantations. The Prosecutor Vyshinsky accused them of having fomented a plot against the leaders of the Party; of having, with the help of Trotsky (who was associated successively in the trials with the Left, the Centre and the Right (which shows a splendid eclecticism)) set up a terrorist centre which had assassinated Kirov; of having planned the assassination of Stalin, Voroshilov and other leaders of the Party. Having obligingly confessed to all the crimes of which they were accused, with the exception of Smirnov who tried to resist, all the accused were sentenced to death and shot. The official *History of the Communist Party* (b) sums up very precisely the charges held by the Party against its former leaders:

Brought before the court were Zinovyev, Kamenev, Bakayev, Yevdokimov, Pikel, I. Smirnov, Mrachkovsky, Ter Vaganian, Reingold and others. Caught red-handed, the criminals had to acknowledge publicly before the court that not only had they planned the assassination of Kirov, but that they had also prepared that of all the other leaders of the Party and of the government. The cross-examination later established that these criminal scoundrels had also engaged in acts of diversion and of espionage. The most monstrous moral and political degeneracy, the vilest cowardice and treachery disguised under hypocritical protestations of loyalty to the Party were revealed in the Moscow trials in 1936 in these men.

The inspirer and main organiser of this whole gang of assassins and spies was the Judas, Trotsky. He had as aides and as executors of his counter-revolution directives Zinovyev, Kamenev and their Trotskyist henchmen ... They had become the despicable servants and agents of Germano-Polish fascists.

During their trial some of the accused had implicated Bukharin, Tomsky and Rykov and the Prosecutor Vyshinsky announced that proceedings against them were to be taken. Fearing the worst, Tomsky committed suicide on 23 August. Some days later, on 10 September, Vyshinsky announced that the prosecution, having been unable to find legal grounds for the charges against Bukharin and Rykov, the case was closed. This decision seems to show some reluctance on the part of the Party, perhaps influenced by Tomsky's suicide, to proceed with the charges. On 26 September, Stalin and Zhdanov telegraphed from Sochi to Kaganovich, Molotov and other members of the Politburo that it was 'absolutely necessary and urgent that Comrade Yezhov be appointed to the position of People's Commissar of the Interior. Yagoda has shown himself completely incapable of unmasking the Trotskyist-Zinovyevist bloc. In this matter the GPU is lagging four years behind.' Happier in his duties than his predecessor, Yezhov set up another trial and gave his name to the period of terror.

The second great trial took place in January 1937. There were seventeen accused, among them Piatakov, Radek, Sokolnikov, Serebryakov, Muralov. The charge against them was to some extent more subtle than those which had been raised against their predecessors, closer above all to the immediate problems of the Soviet Union. Like their predecessors, they were accused of having plotted with Trotsky, but this time the object of the plot was the destruction of the Soviet Union. Having set up a reserve centre destined to replace that of Zinovyev, the accused had betrayed the Party, but also their motherland, selling themselves to foreign Powers, above all to Germany and Japan, sabotaging the economy. These were subtle charges because Soviet public opinion was at the time sensitive about two subjects, the German danger and the economic difficulties. Piatakov, accusing himself of having sabotaged the carrying out of the Plan, confirmed once again the Stalinist thesis that the policy carried out by the Party was correct, and that any weakness was due only to treason. Thirteen of the accused were condemned to death and executed. Among those who escaped, Sokolnikov and Radek were given ten years in prison. The trial had been largely dominated by the brilliant personality of Radek who played a very ambiguous starring part in it, accusing himself and others (the year before he had demanded with Piatakov the death penalty for Zinovyev and Kamenev), he seemed at the same time to be constantly accusing the whole regime. At the end of the trial, it was said of him that he was 'a demon, but not a man'.

Once again, during the trial Bukharin and Rykov were implicated. However, a whole year went by until they in turn appeared before the court. In this interval, calm seemed to have returned to judge by appearances and in the February Plenum the Central Committee discussed election to the Supreme Soviet and democracy in the Party. However, behind this apparent calm a fierce struggle was raging within the Party over the continuation of the terror. On 17 February 1937 Ordzhonikidze, Stalin's old friend and accomplice, who during the last weeks had clashed with Stalin in order to save his aide Piatakov, his elder brother and his friend Alexis Svanidze, Stalin's brother-in-law, committed suicide in circumstances which are still suspicious.

In the Plenum of the Central Committee (23 February–5 March 1937) Stalin attacked 'the lacuna in the work and methods of the Party for the liquidation of Trotskyists and other hypocrites' and explained that the advance of the Soviet State necessitated an 'aggravation of the class struggle in the country and demanded through this an increased vigilance'. Yezhov gave more details on the extension of the Trotskyist network in the provinces, basing his case on the denunciations provoked by the Party, and the members of the Central Committee who still expressed doubts, such as Postyshev, found themselves on very shaky ground. The Central Committee decided to expel Rykov and Bukharin from the Party and agree that it was necessary in such circumstances to authorise the use of 'methods of physical pressure'. The *yezhovshchina* could be used.

That year (1937) was the year of secret arrests – Bukharin and Rykov were probably already in prison when the Central Committee expelled them – of trials in camera, of hasty and unceremonious executions. The heads of the Red Army – Tukhachevsky, Yakir, Uborevich – were tried and executed in this way and the communiqué on 11 June, which announced their death, was probably published well after the event. Denounced by the press in March for having fomented a fascist military plot, the heads of the Red Army disappeared. After them, the whole leadership of the army had to undergo the ordeal of the process of being interrogated, and here again suicide was often a way out for these despairing men like Gamarnik who killed himself in May 1937.

For the political cadres, the balance-sheet of this anonymous liquidation, the victims of which were often not known until 1956, was also heavy. Kosior, Rudzutak, Eikhe Bubnov, Chubar, Yenukidze and many others, members from the very early days, disappeared in this way. However, the violence of the campaign in the press which demanded that the 'rightist and Trotskyist vipers' be denounced shows that the Party wanted to go far beyond this. In March 1938, the last great trial, that of the 'bloc of anti-Soviet rightists and Trotskyists' marked a new and final stage in the purge. To the bench of the accused hurried, under paradoxical labels, men of every trend, genuine rightists, Bukharin and Rykov, one of the most implacable leaders of the Left, Rakovsky, one of Sverdlov's successors, Krestinsky, the former head of the GPU, Yagoda, two national leaders at the highest level, Khodzhayev and Ykramov, doctors accused of having been paid to kill their co-accused Gorky and his son, Pechkov, Menzhinsky, Kuibyshev and others. As in the past, the shadow of Trotsky hovered over the whole trial. The old leaders of the Party were, like the accused of the previous year, supposed to have betrayed their country by selling themselves to the most varied foreign Powers, to Germany and Japan, as usual, but also to Britain and to Poland. There was one new charge: they had premeditated not only the assassination of the leaders who were still alive, but also that of Lenin. On this point, Bukharin who agreed that he was guilty of many of the crimes, refused obdurately to confess his guilt, to have plotted with the social revolutionaries to bring this about. This incident is very interesting. In fact, by means of this trial Stalin was determined to degrade his adversaries, to discredit them, and to show that they were deviationists. With the trial of 1938 he tried to erase them even from the history of the Party, to show that they had always belonged to the enemy camp. And those who had been forced to bow to Stalin's demands, to confess to unimaginable crimes, recoiled from this last sacrifice and fought to preserve their place in Lenin's Party.

The trial of the rightists too was not lacking in illuminating episodes. In retracting his confession before the court and in stating that it had been forced from him, Krestinsky demonstrated the mechanics of the confessions. The accused who refused to accept that he was guilty of the crimes imputed to him was never given access to a public trial, and in order to explain himself publicly, to proclaim the truth in a place where it could be heard, the accused had first to agree that he was guilty. But what followed the Krestinsky incident showed that the human voice is too weak, even in a court, to be heard, and the judicial machine was too perfect. After forty-eight hours, Krestinsky gave in and retracted all his denials. Similarly, Bukharin adopted a very remarkable attitude, pouring sarcasm on the confessions, destroying in a few words the whole charge but never gaining the advantage, as if there existed behind the skirmishes an implicit rule of the game which forced him to admit his guilt. Like all the trials, that of 1938 was an accumulation of improbabilities, of flagrant counter-truths, of ridiculous details which would make amusing reading were it not for the bloody *dénouement*. Interrogating Zelensky, charged with economic sabotage, Vyshinsky had this extraordinary dialogue with him:

VYSHINSKY: Were there cases in which the members of your organisation, who were concerned in one way or another with the stocking up of butter, put ground glass in butter?

ZELENSKY: There were cases in which ground glass was found in the butter.

VYSHINSKY: Not in which ground glass was *found* in the butter, but was *put* in the butter. You understand the difference; ground glass was put there. Were there such cases or not?

ZELENSKY: There were cases in which ground glass was put in the butter.

VYSHINSKY: Were there cases in which your co-participants, your accomplices in the criminal plot against the Soviet government and the Soviet people, put nails in the butter? . . . and did you not put nails in the eggs?

ZELENSKY: No.

VYSHINSKY: And why not? Because it did not work? The shell prevented you?

These staggering details led to the death sentence and to the immediate execution of the eighteen accused. Alone among the great figures of the trial, Rakovsky, who had at the time half a century of revolutionary activity behind him, escaped capital punishment. He, who was now only a broken old man, was condemned to a life of twenty years in prison and died in a camp during the war.

This trial closed the period of the purges. Even while Vyshinsky was in full cry against the rightists, a reaction, still timid but nevertheless clearly discernible, appeared in the Party. The Plenum of the Central Committee of January 1938 gave proof of the widespread fatigue with the uninterrupted purges. For the first time, it was no longer the 'passive' elements which came under the fire of criticism but the 'careerists', who in order to protect themselves or to facilitate their promotion had falsely accused their superiors. The Party suddenly deplored the fact that there had developed within its ranks 'a hard and bureaucratic attitude' towards those who were suspected of being enemies of the people. It is true that for several months still arrests and liquidations continued, but within the Party the signs of change were on the increase. The number of expulsions decreased, measures of clemency, even of rehabilitation, were taken on behalf of the expelled, the recruitment of new members became easier. On a broader level, the institutions also reflected this change. Beriya was appointed in July beside Yezhov, then in December 1938 he succeeded him as the head of the NKVD – a significant change if the role played by Yezhov and his reputation is recalled. On 20 January 1939 Stalin addressed to the secretaries of the regional organisations of the Party and the officers of the NKVD a circular prolonging the use of 'physical pressure, in exceptional cases against the notorious and impenitent enemies of the people' but this was a general threat rather than a renewal of the terror: slowly the country returned to normal.

BALANCE-SHEET OF THE TERROR

After the turmoil of the years 1929–33, the purges had enclosed the Soviet society in a climate of permanent terror and despair. How can the human losses in these years be assessed, in which fears, despotism and insecurity dominated the lives of individuals? In spite of Khrushchev's revelations at the XXth Congress, in spite of the attempts of Soviet historians at the time, no one has as yet made the exact reckoning of the victims which marked the period of the establishment of Stalinism. The statistical data, scanty as they are, do however shed a little light on the vastness of the tragedy suffered by the Soviet people. The census of January 1937 had counted 164 million inhabitants of the USSR. The forecasts of the second Five-Year Plan for the same period assessed the population at 180.7 million inhabitants. The deficit of 16.7 million individuals was so appalling that Stalin himself, who was little given to considering the sensibilities of those whom he governed, did not dare to admit it and annulled the census. The figures, already terrible in their dryness, are not adequate to describe those years. They neither describe the fear felt by everyone, nor the despair of the ruined families nor the hunted fate of the children of these 'enemies of the people', abandoned under false identities in orphanages nor the cohorts of the living dead who populated the camps and the prisons. Nor do they speak of the nights in which everyone waited for the knock on the door which tore them away from life and opened on to a terrifying fate; nor the cowardly relief which all felt when the knock fell on the door of a neighbour. They do not describe how this rampant terror affected men's minds and changed their attitudes. Neither Solzhenitsyn, who was the courageous and patient chronicler of this history of a vast collective tragedy, nor novelists like Grossman, Dombrovksy and many others who have tried to reconstruct it piece by piece, have really described it. It goes without saying that it cannot be undertaken here. Here one can only sketch in a broad and schematic outline, a limited balance-sheet of the consequences of the purges on the Party, on the leading circles of the USSR and on the population as a whole.

The cost of these exceptional years is still not sufficiently recognised, in spite of the revelations made at the XXth and XXIInd Congresses by Khrushchev and the attempt by the Soviet historians to paint a real picture of the period. The balance-sheet must be attempted at different levels, that of the Party, of the ruling circles of the USSR, and that of the population as a whole.

As for the Party, the first balance-sheet of the purges was presented by Malenkov at the XVIIIth Congress which was held in 1939. According to Malenkov, out of the 1,589,000 Party members in 1939, only 8.3 per cent had been members before 1920, that is to say, the Old Guard had been completely eliminated. Of the recruits of the years 1920–21, 80 per cent disappeared during the purges; the same fate was reserved for 75 per cent of the members recruited between 1921 and 1928 and for 50 per cent of those who joined the Party in 1929–30. The Party which emerged from the turmoil was really a new Party. This was also true of the leaders, since 70 per cent of the Central Committee elected in 1934 had been physically eliminated.

If one examines the history of these years and tries to ignore the sensational aspect of the great trials, one can see more clearly what the purge was, taken as a whole. Made up of successive waves, each wave seemed to bring repression nearer the centre of power. While the purge of 1933 struck at the rank and file, that is, the almost unpoliticised members convicted of personal defects incompatible with the life of the Party, the procedure of 1935 – verification and exchange of cards – this time concerned the small and medium cadres, that is the politically conscious communists, charged with complicity with the great oppositional centres. In the third wave, finally, the *yezhovshchina* was unleashed against the ruling cadres and the intelligentsia of the Party, which until then had shared power with Stalin, had sometimes fought and sometimes supported him, but which made up the entire political élite of the Soviet Union. At each stage in these purges the accusers of yesterday became the accused. Stalin had always, in the period of his ascent to power as well as in that of the purges, excelled in inciting his adversaries against each other in order that they should destroy themselves while he assumed the role of arbiter or victim. Was there any reasoning behind this coherent engineering of the purges? Was it part of a definite plan? Or was it an uncontrolled chain of events . . .?

Shaumyan stated that Stalin met with strong opposition in the Central Committee in 1934 and Khrushchev confirmed this several times, linking it to the assassination of Kirov. In 1936, the telegram sent by Stalin and Zhdanov said that the police were four years behindhand in the purging activity which seems to point directly to the period in which the purges of the Party began. In the light of these facts, it would seem likely that a vast purge had been envisaged and that the early purges of the Party had had the effect, among others – perhaps also with an end in mind but this has not been proved – of making possible, with the help of fear, the final fury of the years 1937–38.

One of the questions which must be answered in this context is whether the purges were approximately the same for all the national and regional groups of the Union. Or were some regions affected or spared? In absolute figures, it appears that no group was affected in particular and that the repression was general throughout the whole territory of the Soviet Union. However, the results of the purges were particularly damaging for the non-Russian peoples of the Union, the greater part of whose national cadres disappeared in the turmoil.

Until the 1930s, the Soviet regime had kept an equal balance between the ill-effects of Great Russian chauvinism and the national deviations. The purges of the years 1933–38 were, in the non-Russian lands, to be directed essentially against national manifestations and were intended to destroy the whole national élite in power, all those who were suspected of wanting to limit the central government's hold over their republic. On 7 July 1933, Skrypnik, one of the founders of the Ukrainian Communist Party, who had recently been appointed Vice-President of the Council of Peoples' Commissars of the Republic and President of the Planning Commission, had been driven to suicide. *Pravda* (8 July 1933) wrote that this communist, who had joined the party in 1897, had not behaved like a true communist and had turned towards petit-bourgeois nationalism. At the same time, the President of the Central Executive Committee of Tadzhikistan, Maksum Nuzratallah, and the President of the Council of Peoples' Commissars of Tadzhikistan, Khodzhibayev, disappeared; two years later, in 1935, the President of the Council of Peoples' Commissars of Karelia, Dr Gylling also vanished.

At the height of the *yezhovshchina* nearly all the important national leaders were executed. The Presidents of the Council of Peoples' Commissars of Azerbaizhan (Musabekov), of Byelorussia (Goldred), of Georgia (Mgaloblishvili), of Kazakhstan (Isayev), of Kirghizia (Isakayev), of Tadzhikistan (Rakhimbayev), of Turkmenia (Atayev), of Uzbekistan (Khodzhayev), as well as the Vice-Presidents of the Central Executive Committees of Azerbaizhan (Effendyev), of Kazakhstan (Kulumyetov), of Kirghizia (Vrazbyekov), of Tadzhikistan (Shotemar), of Turkmenia (Aitakov), of Uzbekistan (Akhun Babayev). In Byelorussia their equivalent Chervyakov committed suicide in 1937 as did also the president of the Ukrainian Sovnarkom, Lyubchenko. From the higher echelons of the Party, Ikramov, First Secretary of the Uzbekistan Party, the Kazakhs Sadvokazov, Ryskulov, Seyfullin; great national writers like the Uzbeks Fitrat, Cholpan, Munnever Qari all disappeared in the maelstrom. Even the former President of the Azerbaizhan Sovnarkom Narimanov, who had died in 1933, was posthumously condemned as a 'bourgeois deserter and nationalist'.

In Armenia, the Party leadership was subjected to a ruthless purge after the plot of the 'Dashnak secret organisation' had been uncovered. It was accused of having wanted to overturn the Soviet regime and to replace it by a bourgeois regime, supported by foreign powers. The leaders of the Armenian Party, Kahnshian, Ter Gabrielian, etc. were then executed. As in the rest of the Soviet State it was not only the leaders, but also the entire apparatus of the national parties which was purged. The Ukraine which, by 1933, had already lost half its regional secretaries, underwent a second purge, as widespread as that of 1938. In Georgia, 260 out of 300 secretaries were eliminated.

The purges thus can be seen to have had two unfavourable consequences for these parties. First of all, the liquidation of the higher cadres meant that the republics were deprived of almost their entire national élite which had emerged from the national movements of 1917 and that a new more malleable generation, with Soviet training, took their place. The second was that the purges brought to an abrupt end the movement of *indigenisation* of the national parties which had been underway since the beginning of the 1930s, following the recruitment which took place at that time. From January 1931 to April 1932, the proportion of national communists in the 34 principal non-Russian organisations had risen from 50.9 per cent to 53.8 per cent. The situation of the later years is only known for the Communist Parties of the Ukraine, Kazakhstan and the three Central Asian republics, but it would seem that it could be extended to all the other non-Russian republics. For these republics, an examination of the statistical data shows everywhere a fall in the number of local inhabitants between 1933 and 1937, followed by a more or less genuine recovery after 1938. Although the Ukrainians succeeded in 1940 in almost reaching the level of 1933, the same was not true of the other peoples who remained markedly behind (Uzbeks, 61% in 1933 and 50% in 1940; Tadzhiks, 53% and 45%; Kirghizs 59% and 44% in 1941). For all that, the indigenisation of the Ukrainian Communist Party (UCP) was only a relative success because, during the same period, the Party's recruitment policy in the USSR led to a greater preponderance of Russians in the Party as a whole. The Ukrainians, who were privileged compared with the other peoples when seen at the local level, did not succeed in regaining their position at the federal level. Representing 21.2 per cent of the Soviet population, out of which the communists represented 13 per cent of the total Party in 1933, the Ukrainians only provided 11 per cent in 1940.

The years of organised terror brought to completion in many respects the transformation of Soviet society started in 1938. In the first stage 1928–33, the vast mass of peasants were uprooted from their customs and their way of life and forcibly thrown into structures which had been designed to train and remodel them. During the same period, through the demands of collectivisation and of the Plan, a first assault was launched against what was specific to the peoples, imposed sometimes for economic reasons but mainly by the determination to unify and centralise. The USSR of the first Plan had to move towards the obliteration of social, but also of national, differences and not of their assertion, which is something that too often tends to be overlooked. The political objectives of the economic planning were often resisted and the wave of purges between 1933 and 1938 was designed to reduce the resistance, in that it helped Stalin to rid himself of his open adversaries. A final assessment of the purges clearly illuminates their meaning and aim and, in the last resort, their relative coherence. Millions of anonymous men and women were torn from their homes during these years and thrown into camps on the strength of a simple denunciation. But the intended victims of those years were above all those who had links with the sources of power. The anonymous citizen was less directly threatened than was the communist member of the rank and file or the Party cadres. The same was true of the non-Russian peoples where the purges first of all struck at the political cadres and the intelligentsia, sparing those who took no part in political life. Generally, the non-political victims were attacked in the name of the demands of economic efficiency.

To complete this assessment, several questions arise about the means which the divided leadership of the Party used to impose its policy on its adversaries and on the whole country. Many authoritarian regimes have in the course of history imposed their authority on nations, but in general they imposed it by means of an all-powerful body – the army or Party. In the Soviet Union, on the contrary, the small team which had survived the terror – Stalin, Molotov, etc. – had been at the centre of a divided leadership which it had decimated, at the summit of a Party which it had purged again and again throughout the whole period, with an army which it had also subjected to devastating purges. No class being free from the terror, what was the power base of the Stalinist team?

It appears that the team benefited not from the instruments of power, but from negative elements: the neutrality of the army, the fear of the Party and the passivity of the country.

The problem of the army at that time was extremely important because the events of 1935–38 showed a type of special relationship between the army and the State and so influenced the political future of the USSR.

At no time, neither during the violence of collectivisation nor in the years of the purge, did the army show any desire to resist the authorities nor to influence them, although it was, involved in both of these episodes. The Red Army was essentially peasant in origin (in 1926, 11% of the soldiers were of peasant origin as against 18% of working class origin) and it might be supposed that the fight begun in 1928 against the peasantry would not have left it indifferent. From 1934 on, the purges of the Party also affected the army to the extent that it contained a high proportion of communists (37% in 1927, representing 50% of the officers' corps) and in which after 1937 the military cadres were in turn purged. Many memoirs of Soviet military leaders explain the attitude of the army which throughout these events remained aloof from the conflicts and passively accepted the blows dealt to it. The explanation is to be found in the particular situation of the army of 1925 and also in the particular forms taken by the purge of the army. Having surmounted the period of hesitation as to whether there should be a proletarian militia or a regular army, the Soviet army after 1924 was a permanent army whose powers as a constituted body were to be continuously strengthened. Controlled by the Party, the army was gradually to extricate from this control a personal authority, that of the officers.

In 1935, while the Party was rocked by the purges, the army was benefiting from increasing advantages: the re-establishment of military ranks, the growing authority of its leaders and the development of an autonomous military education. The evolution which had been taking place since 1924 took definite shape, and the army became a privileged, homogeneous, socially inward-looking body. The time-table of the purges reveals the government's concern not to disorientate the army. In 1934, whereas 12 per cent of the leading members of the Party had already been eliminated, the purges only affected 3 per cent of the military cadres. It was not until 1937 that the purge of the army began and even so it was still limited to the top ranks. The 35,000 uniformed victims of the purges represented over half the officer corps. Among them the higher ranking officers paid a very heavy price: the liquidation affected 3 out of 5 Soviet marshals, 13 army commanders out of 15, 57 corps commanders out of 80, 70 divisional commanders out of 190, the 11 vice-commissars for war, 75 out of the 90 members of the Higher Council for War. The entire military leadership was decimated.

But at once a new team appeared, very different from the eliminated military cadres. It was composed of young officers trained in the military schools since 1930. The purge of the army enabled the veterans of the Civil War to be replaced by a new generation. Like the Party, the army took on a new look. But its rank and file, almost unaffected by the purges, solidly structured by the political commissariats which reappeared in 1937 after a long eclipse, freely attributed the misfortunes of the leaders to the fact that many of them were not of lowly birth. This was clearly stated by the Soviet General Gorbatov, who himself was of peasant origin, although this did not prevent him from being arrested in 1938. Hearing in 1937 of the discovery of a 'military plot' which led to the liquidation of Tukhachevsky, he commented:

The news has stunned me. How is it possible, I ask myself, that men who have played a leading role in the defeat of the foreign armies of intervention and of those of the counter-revolutionaries at home, men who have done everything to perfect our army, who showed that they themselves were communists at every test during the terrible years, how could these same men have become enemies of the people? Finally, after having reflected on all the possible solutions, I came to the most widely held at the time: 'What is bred in the bone will come out in the blood.' This saying had an apparent foundation of truth in that Tukhachevsky and some of the others who were arrested with him came from a wealthy background.

The memoirs of General Gorbatov also show clearly how the army – and even those of its members who were arrested and escaped – was aware in this period that the army was an exceptional social corps which should be protected. When this situation was not threatened, the army remained neutral and did not give the political power any problems.

As regards the Party, the question of its attitude appeared at two levels, that of the leaders and that of the rank and file. As far as the leaders were concerned, it is difficult to understand at first glance how the Bolshevik Old Guard agreed, without much resistance, to incriminate itself, to accuse itself of crimes which it had not committed and to go to their deaths. The former denials had a logic which Radek had expressed: Stalin's companions thought that because of their recantations they would be able to stay in the Party in order to change it, to fight effectively within it against Stalin's authority or to help the policy that they advocated to succeed. But after 1936, things were no longer the same; their confessions and their self-criticism could only alienate them still further from the Party. It is unthinkable that simply the idea of saving their lives guided these men who had always sacrificed themselves for the revolutionary cause. In no case can personal interests be invoked. On the contrary, two, probably complementary, explanations, are suggested both by the past of the Bolsheviks and by what we know about the purges. First of all, there was the moral and physical pressure.

The spectacle offered by Rakovsky who, in the witness-box appeared simply as a ruin of a man, and the about-turns of Krestinsky were signs of physical pressure. But, above all, there was the moral pressure to which these men were subjected, the appeal in the first place to family loyalty. The courageous insolence of a Bukharin, who demolished the system of accusation and then allowed Vyshinsky to reconstruct imperturbably the charges which he had just shown to be absurd, gives a glimpse of innumerable bargains.

Over and above these immediate pressures, another loyalty certainly helped to dictate the attitude of the Old Guard, the loyalty which linked it to the Party. In 1936–38, the German threat to the USSR was taking visible shape, and the country was disorganised. It is probable that over and above their personal attachments, the old Bolsheviks once again considered that the unity of the Party was at stake, that by taking on themselves all the errors and weaknesses of the Party, their sacrifice would unite the masses around the leaders who had not failed. As for the rank and file of the Party and even the whole of the country, their passivity was understandable if one looks at the whole period and the totality of the process of the purges. Repression and liquidation of the leaders were not achieved all at once, but were the result of a very subtle gradation. The rank and file of the Party, the masses, after watching over the years the old Bolsheviks admitting their errors, their deviations, hailing the party leadership – which became more and more identified with Stalin – as the repository of truth, had to transfer all their confidence and their loyalty to Stalin alone. From accusations to confessions, from internal quarrels to denunciations, the whole of the Old Guard was itself dishonoured and discredited and was used to show the masses that its members admitted that they had betrayed the incorruptible leader, Stalin. The charisma that Stalin tried to inject into the political life of the USSR on Lenin's death was handed to him by his opponents, cleverly manipulated to this end. They seem only to have understood this very belatedly.

Finally, the essential political consequence of the process of purges undertaken in the 1930s was that a new political system was set up in the USSR. This political system was characterised by the absolute power of one man, relying on a police apparatus which recognised no other authority than Stalin's. However, Stalin's total power had complex aspects which strengthened it and bewildered his adversaries. Above all, this was true of his relations with the Party. While systematically setting out to destroy the Party, by placing it under the control of the repressive apparatus, Stalin always preserved appearances and declared that he was simply the servant of a Party which he dominated and destroyed. In the same way, he declared that he alone among all the old Bolsheviks was Lenin's heir, the continuer of his work, and he forced his colleagues through their confessions and recantations to acknowledge this claim. In a few years Stalin was to use for his own ends – the building of his own power – the system and the ideas bequeathed by Lenin and the various existing political and police apparatuses which he remodelled and manipulated.

This was true also of the nature of his relations with society. Architect of an unprecedented terror, Stalin was not always seen as such. Although the poet Mandelstam denounced in him the 'man-eater', the terrorised society sometimes saw in him their last refuge against an arbitrariness, which it had difficulty in locating. The Smolensk archives give examples of this misunderstanding. During the terror, people who felt threatened by the police, who had suffered, sometimes addressed moving pleas to Stalin asking for his protection against the violence and the injustice. He was then the supreme arbiter, but also the protecting Father from whom help was expected.

Stalin derived his legitimacy both from the confessions of his adversaries whom he destroyed and from his ambiguous relations with the bewildered masses. Bewildered they were, all the more because Stalin's policy of terror led to the atomisation of Soviet society. During these years, the Soviet ruler was confronted only by individuals isolated in their anxiety and not by groups which could exert pressure. The purges had taught society that, when face to face with power, they were protected neither by their own kind nor by the institutions. On the contrary, the mutual distrust, the fear of being compromised had isolated every individual. This social atomisation was a decisive help to Stalin's power which was able from then on to grow unhindered.

Chapter four

THE EVE OF BATTLE

Between 1934 and 1938, the acceleration of the purges had fixed everyone's attention on the political upheavals in the USSR and on the dramas which were being played out there. These spectacular events disguised the profound changes which were taking place at the same time in the country. It was only when calm returned that the gulf separating the USSR of 1938 from that of the end of the 1920s could be measured and it was above all the war that was to reveal how deep these changes were. Two elements were fundamental in this respect: the evolution of the ideology which led to a complete rehabilitation of the State, noted in the Constitution, and the moral transformation of Soviet society, especially of political society.

THE REHABILITATED STATE

What was the nature of the State in 1938?

Until 1934, the survival of the propertied classes in the USSR at least among the peasantry was used as the justification for the growth of a State, whose transitional function was to guarantee the dictatorship of the proletariat and the gradual elimination of the kulaks. After 1934, it was clear that this justification for the maintenance of the State based on the existence of antagonistic classes had vanished and that the Soviet State, in consequence, had to enter into the phase of withering away. But the prevailing situation made it impossible for this evolution to take place because the instability created in the USSR by the purges stood in the way of any coherent evolution of the State. However, it was not only internal events in the USSR which had led to the maintenance of the

State, because this evolution had been taking its course for years. The problem of the future of the State had been formulated on the eve of the Revolution by Lenin in the only theoretical work he devoted to the subject, *The State and the Revolution*. But this text, written in Finland during the feverish weeks which preceded the final assault is extraordinary ambiguous and one can, according to one's preferences, see in it, either an anarcho-syndicalist conception of the State in which 'the cook' will carry out all the extremely simplified tasks or a highly organising and rationalised conception of a State seen 'as a vast office and an immense workshop'.

The contradiction revealed in *The State and the Revolution* is confirmed in another of Lenin's writings, a notebook entitled *Marxism and the State* in which he jotted down what he had gleaned from his reading on the subject. Having reflected for a long time on the viewpoints of the founders of Marxism (essentially the *Critique of the Gotha Programme* and Engels' letter to Bebel), Lenin had pinpointed the differences between them. Engels had replaced the notion of the State by that of the community (*Gemeinwesen*) while Marx evoked the political form of the communist society (*Staatswesen*). Lenin solved the contradiction in his notebook by insisting on the idea of two stages of communism, the transitional stage in which the State of Marx's dictatorship of the proletariat would be maintained and the stage of communism in which the State would disappear. It is around this notion of the *period of transition* that Lenin's reflections centred and that ambiguities begin. Lenin clearly said that the task of the Revolution was to destroy not only the bourgeois State, but the State itself.

The State of transition which succeeds the bourgeois State was different in nature because the State machine had to be broken from the beginning because from its origin it contained the process of withering away. Thus, a comparison of the texts suggests that Lenin had tried to reconcile Engels and Marx, to link their visions together and that he maintained in 1907, like Marx, a political form of State control, while holding that the process of withering away had begun from the very beginning. However, in 1918, when he had to deal the practical problems of the working of a political society, Lenin rejected the ideas he had held in 1917 and clashed with Bukharin, deriding his attachment to the 'fairy tale' of the withering away of the State.

In the years 1925–26, the evolution of Lenin's thought on this problem was even more accentuated by his successors who brought an answer to a practical problem which neither Marx nor Lenin had clarified, that of the *duration* of the period of transition. In 1917, the Bolsheviks thought that the period running from the bourgeois State to full communism would, due to the world-wide spread of the Revolution, be very brief. But once the hope of world revolution had retreated, the capitalist world had shown its strength and the Soviet Union had acknowledged its isolation, it became clear that the period of transition had to be a lasting one, that the USSR also was forced to adapt itself to a world in which opposing political systems dominated. Was not a semi-State, in the process of withering away, surrounded by genuine and strong States, doomed? The new character of the period of transition – isolation and duration – forced Lenin and his successors to redefine their conception of the State in this period.

Already in 1926, Stalin had sketched the broad lines of the justification for the maintenance of the State which he clarified in 1929 in an attack on Bukharin. The dominant trait of Soviet evolution in this period, was, for Stalin, the intense development of the class struggle, which implied the existence of a strong State. This trend was confirmed by the theoretical discussions of the jurists who, realising the unexpected length of the period of transition held that the notion of the provisional was perhaps inappropriate and tried to define, more realistically, the juridical content of the State and its implications in international law. The juridical conceptions of Korovin were replaced in the last years of the 1920s by those of Pashukanis who tried to reconcile the principles and the practice of the Soviet State. If, in the beginning, his ideas were still dominated by the need to defend the idea of a State of transition, after 1934, the foundations of Soviet law were modified. In 1934, the class struggle having been won, the USSR entered upon a new phase of its development. Stalin confirmed this in November 1936, when he presented the draft Constitution. He declared that: 'Our Soviet society has by and large already achieved socialism in the essential; it has created the socialist order, that is, it has reached what the Marxists call the first phase, or the phase inferior to communism.' In these conditions, the State had lost its former justification and had to enter the final phase of withering away. Nevertheless, Stalin at this time set out the problem in a new fashion and opened the way to the rehabilitation of the State. For him, the absence of the class war within the country was not a fundamental fact because the class war was to take place in future on a world scale, opposing the Soviet socialist State and the capitalist States. The future of the State was not, therefore, determined by the internal evolution of the USSR, but it was the persistence of the capitalist encirclement which made it necessary to maintain and even to strengthen the State. The jurists flew to Stalin's aid to draft a law which would be the law of this decisive phase in the confrontation of the two antagonistic political systems.

In the course of lectures which he gave at the Party Institute for the Construction of the Soviet State and the Law, Pashukanis put the finishing touches to the rehabilitation of the State which he had outlined some years before. He attacked the jurists of the transitional school for the contempt in which they held the State, and stated that the proletarian State was the sole subject of law, that it could not be confused with the 'conscience' of the proletariat. The difference between the proletarian State and the political or trades union organisations of the proletariat must not be blurred, he wrote. The reaffirmation of the juridical and moral personality of the State was accompanied by a recognition of the classic attributes of the State, and in the first place of the notion of the State-controlled territory: 'The territory is the domain of spatial expansion of sovereignty.' This State-controlled conception of the State seemed to be completely contrary to the revolutionary dynamism which in the beginning had inspired the young Soviet State, the starting point of revolution in the world. And the Soviets, in fact, had tried to differentiate between the Soviet State, a stable and defined State, and the Comintern, the world party of the Revolution.

However, Pashukanis had, while rehabilitating the State, kept open the possibility of the later withering away by basing his whole theory on the balance of power in the world, hence the totality of the system had only a relative value. It was against this relativism that there arose the school led by Vyshinsky, which, in 1936, eliminating Pashukanis, perfected the evolution of ideas. For Vyshinsky, law was in every circumstance 'the expression of the will of the ruling class'; thus, in the socialist State, it expressed the will of the proletariat supported, the antagonistic contradictions having disappeared from within the society, by the whole society. It was, thus, in the last resort, the expression of the general will. Hence, the law acquired a permanent character and so did the State, through which it regulated social relations. The idea of the withering away of the State was thus relegated to one side in favour of this permanence, at least so long as the capitalist encirclement lasted. The Constitution of 1936 reflected this ideological evolution because, unlike the former constitutions, it defined a State fixed in space and in time, a State which corresponded to the international norms and through doing so took its place in the international community; a State that affirmed itself as the successor to the Tsarist State, because the transformation of the social structure and the political change had not destroyed according to Vyshinsky and his colleagues, the continuity of the State.

This evolution, which was noted in the Constitution, was inevitable for two reasons. On the internal plane, the immensity of the tasks with which the Bolshevik leaders had been confronted since 1917 made the existence of an organised State a necessity. On the external plane, the changes which had taken place in the international situation at the beginning of the 1930s also favoured the maintenance of the State. Threatened by the expansionist aims of Nazi Germany, the USSR could only defend its territorial cohesion by attaching it once again to a generally accepted concept, that of the State and its sovereignty. In defining a spatially stable State, the USSR doubtless forfeited the right to extend the revolutionary area to other countries; but, after 1930, it was clear that the Soviet Union had to defend itself against German expansion rather than to think about its own territorial expansion. The German threat, which implied an aggravation of the capitalist encirclement, justified the Stalinist insistence on the strengthening of the State, but the rehabilitation of the State was in process before this threat appeared. In 1939, Stalin explained to the XVIIIth Congress the idea no longer of the maintenance but of the necessary strengthening of the State.

He said that in the particular and concrete case of the victory of socialism in one country alone taken separately, surrounded by capitalist countries, threatened by military aggression from outside, that country must have a sufficiently strong State to defend the gains of socialism against external attacks; he went on to say that the State should maintain itself even when the stage of communism had been completely reached if capitalism continued to exist anywhere, if the slightest external threat existed.

THE CONSTITUTION OF 1936

The Constitution of 1936, important because it genuinely marked the almost unlimited restoration of the State, did not make any modifications in the fundamental principles of the regime: federal organisation, role of the Party and system of public liberties. Article 126 of the Constitution defined the place and the guiding role of the Party in the political and social life of the USSR; Article 125 laid down that the fundamental freedoms – freedom of speech, of the press, of assembly, of public meetings – were guaranteed by the law 'in conformity with the interests of the workers and with a view to affirming the socialist system'. This formula indicated the limits of public liberties, but no text, either in the Constitution or elsewhere, explained what were the effective guarantees which accompanied the liberties laid down by the Constitution.

The modifications brought by the Constitution of 1936 concerned essentially the territorial organisation of the USSR and the structure of the central representative organs, the right to vote and the description of the economic and social base of the USSR. The Constitution modified the structure of the central representative organs. The Congress of Soviets and the Central Executive Committee were replaced by a Supreme Soviet, made up of two Chambers, the Soviet of the Union, the Soviet of the nationalities. The Soviet of the Union was to be elected by all the citizens of the USSR with one deputy for every 300,000 inhabitants; the Soviet of the nationalities was to be elected on the basis of national participation with 25 deputies per federated republic, 11 for each autonomous republic, 5 for each autonomous region, 1 for each national district.

The number of federated republics was increased from seven to eleven as a consequence of the creation of two republics, Kazakhstan and Kirghizia, and the division of the SSR of Transcaucasia into three republics, Armenia, Georgia, Azerbaizhan.

Article 134 substituted direct and secret suffrage for the restricted and indirect suffrage of 1924. The right to put forward candidates was restricted to the social organisations: the Party, trades unions, co-operatives, etc. The political base of the USSR was defined as one of Soviets of workers' deputies (Article 2); the economic base was 'constituted by the socialist economic system and the socialist ownership of the tools and means of production' (Article 4). The plan of the State 'determining and guiding the economic life of the USSR' (Article 11). Thus the Constitution took note of the social change which had taken place since 1928.

The Constitution, however, did not reveal another important change – that of the rehabilitation during the same time of the national values.

THE REHABILITATION OF THE NATION

Since the beginning, as we have seen, the nation had preoccupied the Bolsheviks more than the other European socialists and, confronted by the national problems which were entangled with the class war in Russia, they had opted for a solution which would, they hoped, enable a higher level of consciousness to be reached, that of true internationalism. Although for some years during the 1930s the Soviet regime had claimed to be a society based on class consciousness and not on the national consciousness, from the beginning of the 1930s an ideological change in this respect could be discerned, which was to lead to the rehabilitation of the nation under various forms: national consciousness, historical consciousness and patriotism.

The appearance of a collective national consciousness can be situated round about 1934–35. This change came about because of external factors and Nazi Germany certainly played a great part in it. Hitler never concealed his ambitions as regards the East and his coming to power presented a threat to the USSR of which after 1933–34 it was constantly aware. Hitler's objective was not the destruction of the Soviet regime; it was above all the acquisition of the lands belonging to the USSR and the reduction of the Slav peoples to the ranks of producers in the service of the Germans. His vision of German-Soviet relations was a classic colonialist one and this vision created a reaction in defence of the nation because it was the integrity of the Soviet nation which was at stake. The internationalist and revolutionary conception symbolised by the existence of the Comintern and the holding of congresses which periodically reminded the world that a world revolution was taking place gave way to a defensive conception based on the national will and the national interests.

Towards 1934 the first signs of the development of the collective national consciousness could be seen in the USSR. Two forgotten expressions at that time reappeared in the press, which had been abandoned precisely because of their national, instead of their socialist, overtones: *Russia* and the *motherland*. These expressions affirmed in a particularly difficult period that together with political and social interdependence there existed another type of interdependence rooted in a common ethnic origin. The attachment of the Soviet citizen to his native soil, to his past was suddenly legitimated. This trend was strengthened by two elements. On the one hand, in the struggle against the opposition during the same period there were frequent denunciations of *cosmopolitanism* based on 'national origins alien to Russia'. The Bolshevik Party suddenly forgot that it was an extraordinary crucible of Russians, Germans, Latvians, etc. But it was above all the constitutional debate which did most to confirm and accelerate this trend.

The Constitution of 1936 was a constitution of a State which was not only the transitional State created by Lenin in 1917, but was fundamentally an enduring State, corresponding to a very old historical reality. During the discussion, *Izvestia* emphasised the historical background of the Soviet State, inviting the Soviet citizens to become familiar with the past history of their country in order to love it more.

The rehabilitation of Russian history was in fact a fundamental aspect of this resurrection of the national principle. During the years following the Revolution, the Bolsheviks had completely obliterated the past history of the USSR and encouraged the growth of a new historical conception based on the study of the class struggle and not on the study of the country. 'Profound forces' were described as alone being responsible for the historical dynamic to the detriment of the classic agents of history, and these profound forces were seen in a world perspective, that of the classes on the international scale and not in the perspective of societies organised on the national scale. Until 1932, this conception was that of a whole Soviet school of history dominated by the great historian, Pokrovsky.

In 1932, however, the viewpoint developed by Pokrovsky's school no longer seemed to coincide with the general ideology. In an article in *Proletarskaya Revoliutsya* Stalin inaugurated criticism of this history which quickly was to lead to a complete condemnation. He reproached Pokrovsky and his disciples for their mechanistic interpretation of the historical process and said that they had not referred to the past of the peoples in order to throw light on their present evolution. The following year, the Central Committee began to study a reform of historical studies and even before the war the effects of this were making themselves felt. Chairs in history, no longer social, but national, were re-established; the historical vision of Pokrovsky gave way in published works to a new conception which, without completely linking up with the past, made a clean break with the ideas which had been current up till then. In this revision of history, two aspects were especially important for the strengthening of the national awareness: the re-evaluation of Russian history and the re-evaluation of the past relations between the various peoples of the Soviet Union. The revision of Russian history operated in two directions: the general study of the Russian past, the evaluation of that past in relation to the revolutionary movement and the Revolution. As far as Russian history was concerned, the school of history which imposed itself after the Revolution had tended too consider that nothing that had happened before 1917 was worth studying neither history nor culture. Russian history was for that school a history of reaction, of violence in which the only positive trends which deserved to be remembered were the great, essentially peasant, popular revolts. Towards 1936, the Soviet school of history interested itself not only in these popular movements but also, and even more, in the formation of the Russian State, in those who had been its architects and defenders. The strength of the Russian State became a positive aspect of history in various respects: on the international plane because Russia had served as a European bulwark against the great invasions and by so doing had enabled Europe to develop: on the internal plane because it had led to the Russian Revolution. Seen from this angle, the historians came to give less value than they had done in the past to the popular movements, the results of which seemed to them sometimes to have been far from constructive. In rising up against the autocracy, rebels like Razin or Pugachev, or later intellectuals like the Decembrists had weakened a State which strong sovereigns were trying to nurture. Progress at that time was on the side of the State and the role played by the rebels, wrote the *Istoricheskii Zhurnal* 'even though in most cases they personified the people' was not objectively progressive. The heroes who objectively helped to advance the progress of Russia in its march towards the Revolution were the great sovereigns Alexander Nevsky, Dmitri Donskoy, Peter the Great. Thus the history of the State was re-established. Of course, the historians recognised the negative aspects of the State: excessive power, oppression of the masses; but for them these were outweighed by the need for a strong State.

The link between the past and the Revolution was one of the central problems of the historical revision at the end of the 1930s and Soviet historians tried to solve the problem which had faced the world communist movement since 1917. They sought for the reply, not as their predecessors had done, in the workers' movement itself nor in the genius of Bolshevism, but in the past history of Russia, in the structures of Russian society and in the specific characteristics of its history and people. Thus, oddly enough, the theorists of 1936 joined up with the populists by linking the success of the Revolution with Russia's own heritage. This ideological change was echoed in the themes of the struggle for power. In condemning Trotsky and his theory of permanent revolution, his attachment to world revolution, Stalin emphasised that Trotsky's greatest defect lay in his lack of confidence in the revolutionary capacities of the Russian people.

The rewriting of history even before the war brought with it cultural consequences because the regime tried to imprint the rehabilitated Russian past on the popular awareness. Films, literature, various artistic manifestations tried to popularise the knowledge of history. In 1937–38, as well as the films devoted to the heroes of the Revolution, *Peter the Great* revived in a still barbaric Russia the image of a great sovereign; above all, *Alexander Nevsky*, the incomparable achievement of Eisenstein, is a veritable page of patriotic history, the epic of the Christian princes driving back barbarism. Alexander Nevsky the saviour of Russia, appeared as the apostle of historic progress, as the representative also of a genuinely Russian history, charged with grandeur and no longer with barbarism and whose place in Europe was already marked. During the same period after the production of Glinka's opera 'A Life for the Tsar', the imperial anthem was played. The State Publishing House reissued Tolstoy. Finally, the government solemnly commemorated the 125th anniversary of the battle of Borodino in 1936 and saluted the great war leaders Suvorov and Kutuzov. This was a far cry from the clean sweep of the 1920s.

However, this reassessment of Russia's historical past was not concerned only with Russia's relations with foreign Powers, but touched above all on the historical relations between the Russian nation and the subject peoples of the Empire, and because of this the problem of the national past of the other peoples of the USSR was evoked.

Until 1930, the official position of the historians was clear on this point. Pokrovsky had summed it up clearly in 1929 at the First Conference of Marxist Historians when he said: 'In the past we Russians – and I am one hundred per cent Great Russian – we were the worst gangsters imaginable.' For Pokrovsky, the foundation of Russian power was colonialism and the Tsarist colonial Empire, the worst in history, had been built upon violence and aggression. 'The prison of the peoples' was one of the characteristics of Russian power long before the Empire of the Romanovs, since he already applied this expression to the reign of Ivan Kalita (1326–41). Fierce in his denunciation of Russia's past, Pokrovsky refused to credit it with any extenuating circumstance or any civilising mission. Its conquests had been simply acts of violence; later the Empire was purely forced and humiliating exploitation of peoples seen only as slaves. Pokrovsky compared this systematic cruelty with the British domination in India. Presented in this way, the colonial system must naturally engender a fierce resistance among its victims. To be sure, the resistance movements were, for the most part, the action of local princes, of feudal or religious leaders, who dragged behind them popular armies, often united by the appeal to national liberation seen as a holy war. Nevertheless, in spite of the fanatically religious character of the resistance movements, in spite of the lack of any proletarian base, the Soviet historians of the first years glorified them and described them as a democratic struggle for liberation. The great heroes of the national resistance of the Caucasus – the Iman Shamil – or of Central Asia – Khan Kennesary Kasy – were thought of as leaders of a progressive movement in the unequal fight against the Russians who were compared to Tamerlane or to Genghis Khan.

This emphasis made it possible for the local historians of all the non-Russian groups to devote themselves for several years to the study of their history, while for the Russians such study was forbidden; it helped to develop already very strong national loyalties. The rehabilitation of the Russian past begun by Soviet ideology towards 1930 was ill-adapted to the maintenance of these extreme theses on colonialism in the relations between the Russians and the non-Russians. Moreover, the Communist Party, which at that time began an open struggle against the nationalist tendencies which prevailed everywhere on the periphery, could scarcely allow the local histories to continue to stress their national pasts, what separated the peoples of the USSR and not what united them.

Thus there began a profound revision of the history of the relations between the Russians and the non-Russians. It concerned first of all Pokrovsky's theories on Russian colonialism. Although the condemnation of colonialism was preserved, its description was watered down. It was not true, said the revised history, that the colonialist behaviour of the Russian State had been worse than that of the other European States. Above all, the conclusions which could be drawn from the existence of the colonial reality were altered. For the historians writing in the 1930s, colonialism had nevertheless been presented as a positive benefit to the conquered peoples, bringing them under the domination of Russia which was the first to make the Revolution and thus enabling them to reap the benefits of the Revolution as early as 1917. Moreover, it often represented for those peoples a lesser evil than any of the other dominations which threatened them at the time. Thus the idea was forged that colonialism had not been an *absolute* evil as Pokrovsky claimed, but a *relative* one. Here again appears the expression of the reformist position defended at the Stuttgart Congress of the Second International by socialists like Bernstein or David who said that colonialism could lead to the progress of the colonised peoples and as such should be accepted. Although Russian domination represented only a relative evil, it was clear that the movements or resistance against Russia were not perhaps as useful and praiseworthy as had been thought hitherto. This change in the assessment of the national histories appeared at the beginning of the 1930s in the attacks launched against the Ukrainian historians. The Communist Party accused them of having continually regarded their past from a purely national angle, while it should have been seen in the light of the class struggle. The great Ukrainian historian Mikhailo Hrushchevsky who for a time directed the Ukrainian Rada was reproached for having insisted on the Ukraine alone, instead of trying to see the positive aspects, creators of the popular co-operation, of the Russo-Ukrainian *rapprochement*. For the first time in 1931 an accusation directed against Hrushchevsky revealed the new ideological orientation. The Ukrainian historian was accused of having, through his excessive nationalism, damaged the Russo-Ukrainian friendship which existed among the peoples.

In 1934, the evolution took definite shape. A common resolution of the Central Committee of the Communist Party and of the Sovnarkom of the USSR insisted on the role the Party ought to play in the definition of history and its teaching. However, on 14 August 1934, the commentaries drafted in common by Stalin, Zhdanov and Kirov on the history textbooks which had been presented to them showed that even at that date the Party had not decided on a general line of history. Although the three leaders were agreed in saying that there must be an end to the specific histories which should be replaced by a concern for the *peoples of the USSR* and not for the *Ukrainians*, the *Moldavians*, etc., they emphasised on the other hand that three elements should not be neglected: the Russian colonialism, that is the simple picture 'Tsarism = prison of the peoples; the counter-revolutionary aspects of the Russian foreign policy of Catherine II at the end of the nineteenth century, that is 'Tsarism, the policeman of Europe'; and lastly the debt owed by the Russian revolutionaries to the European bourgeois and socialist revolutionary movement. This text, the three first points of which were soon to be forgotten, showed that in the summer of 1934 the leaders of the USSR had still not completely revised their ideas and that they still retained much of the vision venerated in the early days of the Revolution.

But as the pace of the internal upheavals quickened, the revision of history began to break with the unfavourable descriptions of the Russian State. In 1937, the publication of an *Abridged Manual of the History of the USSR* by A. D. Shestakov was amended by Zhdanov, the corrections showing the new direction. The Orthodox Church and the monasteries had played, he said, a very positive role in the history of medieval Russia, particularly in bringing to the Slavs 'a written language and some elements of Byzantine culture'; referring to the Ukraine, Zhdanov used the character of Bogdan Hmelnitsky, signatory of the Treaty of Perteyaslev which united the Ukraine to Russia, to develop the idea that this union had been beneficial and that the men who had fought for such unions should be restored to their rightful place, the leading one, in the history of their country. (The Ukrainian historians of the 1920s considered Hmelnitsky at best as an opportunist; Hrushchevsky, Yavorsky and the *Large Soviet Encyclopedia* of 1935 described him as 'a traitor to the Ukrainian people'. Nevertheless Zhdanov stressed that not all rebellions against the imperial power should be seen as beneficial, but should be judged on their merits. This led to the condemnation of the rebellion of the Streltsis against Peter the Great 'who tried to civilise Russia', but did not as yet culminate in the condemnation of the national leaders.

Up to 1939, the truth for the non-Russian peoples lay half-way between two interpretations: colonialism was no longer an absolute evil, but it had to be resisted. In a very peremptory way, the Party invited the national historians to insist more on what united the peoples of the USSR than on what divided them. Stalin intervened personally in 1937, stating that Georgia's passing under the Russian protectorate at the end of the eighteenth century, like the passage of the Ukraine under Russian power, was seen by the authors as an absolute evil, regardless of the concrete historical circumstances of the time. The authors had not realised that at the time two possibilities were open to Georgia – either to be swallowed up by the Shah of Persia or the Sultan of Turkey or to fall under Russian protection, just as the Ukraine had the choice between being absorbed by Pan Poland and the Sultan of Turkey or falling under Russian control. They had not realised that the second possibility represented the lesser evil. Thus, the theory of the *relative evil* or even of the *lesser evil* from then on provided a clear justification. Its effects were different for the Russian people and for the other peoples of the USSR. For the Russians, this theory helped to restore to them an intact historical heritage, which enabled them to regard almost all its aspects with pride. At the same time, it started to dispossess the non-Russians of their past, relativising both their sufferings and their resistance. In the place of this past, of which it gradually deprived a part of its subjects, in place of the national loyalties which it set out to destroy, the Soviet regime tried to create a new loyalty, a new patriotism towards the USSR and the Soviet motherland. But in 1940 this process was still very sketchy and Soviet patriotism based on the common past of the peoples of the USSR tended to be confused with what was Russian.

The rehabilitation of the nation led, at least on the eve of the outbreak of war, to the rehabilitation of the Russian nation, held up as an example; for half the citizens of the USSR, convinced since 1917 by the Soviet rulers themselves that they had been perpetually oppressed by the Russian nation, this was not very convincing. However, the importance of the changes which had taken place in the ideology presented to the popular consciousness should not be underestimated. For the Russians as for the non-Russians, it was the idea of the *nation* which was finally restored; grafted on to that of the State, the political organisation of the nation, it helped to strengthen the idea of the State itself.

To this change in the ideology of the USSR which from internationalist revolutionarism passed to stabilisation within a national framework, must be added another no less fundamental change which took place in the society itself, in which groups and individuals also regained, in their own lives values which broke with those which were honoured in the Leninist epoch.

THE STRATIFICATION OF SOVIET SOCIETY

The problem of the social changes concerns both the ruling class as it emerged from the purges and the relationship of this ruling class with the rest of the Soviet people.

The ruling class in the USSR in 1938 was, above all, the Party, whose members were equally present in the State apparatus; this is why it is necessary to scrutinise carefully the Party as it appeared at that time. We have a clear picture of it, thanks to Molotov's report to the XVIIIth Congress in March 1939, which was both the congress of the return to normal and the congress of assessment of the period which had come to an end. Molotov's report revealed that the Party had been almost completely renewed, that neither historically nor sociologically did it resemble the pre-1934 Party. The history of this Party or rather of its members is a post-revolutionary one as the figures show. Thirty-one per cent of the members of the local committees and 60 per cent of the members of the regional committees present at the Congress were elected to their position for the first time. They had never before been part of the ruling bodies. Eighty per cent of the secretaries of the republics and the regions, 93 per cent of the district secretaries, said Molotov, had joined the Party after 1924, that is they had no experience either of the Revolution or of the Civil War and they had been recruited by the Stalinist Secretariat. Most of these new cadres were under forty. Lenin and his companions in the struggle were for them not living heroes, but heroes they had read about, and they were inclined to accept the Stalinist system which was the only one they had known in the Party. Stalin, besides, confirmed these facts by saying that 500,000 young communists had been promoted to posts of responsibility in the course of the previous three years. What was true of the cadres was also true of the whole of the Party, which, having numbered 3,500,000 members in 1933, had fallen in 1937 to 1,900,000 members, to rise at the time of the XVIIIth Congress to 2,300,000 members and in 1940 to 3,300,000 members. The massive recruitment of the months which followed the end of the purges brought into the ranks of the Party a new generation of communists for whom the history of Bolshevism was purely the history of the Stalinist party.

The post-purge recruitment was above all marked by sociological factors. The XVIIth Party Congress had renewed the appeal for the *proletarisation* of the Party and insisted that priority should be given to the recruitment of workers with five years' employment in production. The rules of the recruitment laid down in 1938 were very different since they invited the Party to open itself to the 'best' (decision of the Central Committee of 14 July 1938), that is 'to the workers, but also to the peasants and the intelligentsia, to people from all sectors of the struggle for socialism'.

The result of the broadening of the base of the Party was a radical change in the sociological composition of the new recruits. If, in 1929, the Party recruited 81 per cent workers, 17 per cent peasants and 1.7 per cent intellectuals, the recruitment of the years 1937–39 brought into the Party 41 per cent workers, 15 per cent peasants,

43.8 per cent intellectuals. The XVIIIth Congress ratified this change by abolishing the directives on 'working class' recruitment which, it said, no longer corresponded to the situation of Soviet society, because the intelligentsia was made up of 'workers and peasants of yesterday and the sons of workers and peasants promoted to responsible positions'.

The change was sociological, but also intellectual, because the number of communists with higher education obviously increased very rapidly. In 1927, the intellectual level of the Party was very low, and this was increased by the massive recruitment of 1927–32. In 1927, 91 per cent of the Party members had only received an elementary education or even no education at all, 7.9 per cent secondary education and 0.8 per cent higher education. Although complete illiterates were rare, one-quarter at least of the members of the Party could only read the letters of the alphabet. This situation was nevertheless more favourable than that in the whole of the rest of the Soviet Union in which, according to the census of 1927, one out of every two citizens over eight years old was still illiterate. Thus, even in the years in which the Party was far from reaching a high intellectual level, it represented the vanguard of the proletariat, but far less than during Lenin's time when the percentage of complete illiterates was 3 per cent. The fact that intellectually the Party was at its lowest during the years 1927–32 should not be forgotten when considering the power struggles, because this element played a very large part. The opposition which made use of the most subtle arguments against Stalin and tried to reason in terms of economic analysis was confronted by the indifference of a Party, in which the majority of the members were incapable of reading and spelling out the texts which were addressed to them. The change which took place in 1939 is particularly striking, compared with this situation. Although four-fifths of the members of the Party had still received only primary education, illiteracy had almost disappeared and, on the contrary, 14.2 per cent of the members had finished a secondary education and 5.1 per cent higher education. This clear improvement corresponded both to the overall progress of education in the Soviet Union (the census of 1939 showed only one illiterate for every five inhabitants of the USSR) and to the emphasis in the Party on a qualitative recruitment.

This new situation (the Party becoming less of a party of workers than in the past) makes it necessary to define the nature and origin of the new Soviet élite which had risen in the Party. Molotov gave some valuable information about this. The Soviet intelligentsia, which was reflected in the Party, he said, represented about 9 to 10 million individuals of which about one-third were to be found in positions of authority in the economy; these new cadres, linked to the transformation of the economic structures of the USSR, supplied a great many of the new recruits to the Party; 1½ to 2 million individuals represented the cadres of the various political and administrative apparatuses. Although Molotov was more vague as to the part of the intelligentsia composed of doctors, teachers, etc., it seems nevertheless to have increased more slowly than the economic and technical intelligentsia and the bureaucratic cadres.

A functional change must be added to the sociological change in the Party reflecting the general change in Soviet society: this was the accelerated growth of the Party's own bureaucracy, through an increase in the number of permanent employees. Although in 1934 the Party numbered around 1 permanent employee for every 20 to 22 members, their number grew in the years of the purges. Stalin stated vaguely in 1938 that the Party contained between 150,000 to 190,000 permanently employed individuals and the most con- servative estimates put the number at about 160,000, which would give 1 employed person for every 15 to 17 members of the Party. This was true of all the apparatuses and the Soviet intelligentsia was increased constantly by the influx of State employees, who played no part in production.

The growth of a privileged élite was only one facet of the Soviet transformation, the other being the parallel deterioration in the conditions of the workers and the stagnation of the condition of the peasants. The end of the purges did not change the status of the working class; on the contrary, the years 1939–40 in which the prospect of war came nearer were studded by a series of measures which restricted still further the freedom of the worker. In view of the economic effort which was speeded up in order to be accom- plished in the short space of time which separated the USSR from a war that Stalin knew was inevitable, a new effort was de- manded of the exhausted workers and to force them to provide it they were imprisoned in laws which strengthened the status set up in 1935–36.

On 20 December 1938 the use of the work-book introduced dur- ing the purges was generalised. This measure was aimed at reduc- ing the mobility of the labour force and of enabling it to be com- pletely controlled. The integration of the worker within the enter- prise was tightened, his dependence on the enterprise was increased. When a worker wanted to leave his workplace the notice was anything from eight days to one month; on the other hand, the conditions in which an enterprise could dismiss a worker became easier, notably through the extension of the main reason for dismissal: unjustified absence. Until 1938, absenteeism presupposed a minimum of a day's absence; a law passed in January 1939 extended this idea to include being twenty minutes late, and four unjustified absences entailed dismissal, with very serious consequences (loss of housing in many cases and of social benefits and difficulty in finding work again).

The social legislation also underwent changes by which the labour force was tied to its place of employment. The sickness benefits which, until 1939, represented the whole of the workers' wages were not, after that year, on a parity with the salary of workers who had spent six years in their enterprise; they fell to 80 per cent of the salary for those who had worked there for between four and six years, 60 per cent for two to three years and 50 per cent for less. The workers thus were tied to their place of employment and were haunted by the fear of dismissal. Two other measures helped to worsen the condition of the worker on the eve of the war. On 26 June 1940 the eight-hour day was reintroduced and unjustified absence was punished by a term of corrective work in the enterprise which brought with it a decrease in wages. The notion of unjustified absence was extended to include the refusal to work overtime in the course of a normal day or of a holiday. Immediately before the war, the average worker was chained to his place of employment and forced to submit to considerable material difficulties. His main problem, at that time, was how to manage his daily life, to ensure his day-to-day existence. A great material insecurity had taken the place of the political insecurity and, among the working class which was underprivileged in the period before the war as among the élite, the concerns of daily life were more important than political fervour. Here again, the ideology appeared essentially in its material aspects.

The situation of the peasants was different, but they could not be said to be a privileged class. The end of the purges had accelereated the return of the peasants to their villages, in which activity centred around the individual plots which were tolerated. The charter of the kolkhozes, promulgated in 1938, tried to harmonise the individual interests of the members of the kolkhoz and the common interest. The rights of the peasants (a plot of 25 to 30 ares, sometimes even a hectare, the possession of a limited number of cattle, sheep and goats and unlimited fowl, the right to sell the produce of his plot on the free market) were guaranteed by Article 7 of the Constitution of 1936. In practice, taking into account the very low prices paid for the obligatory deliveries the kolkhoz had to make to the State, the pre-war period was marked by a remarkable advance in private production. While the individual plots represented barely 3 per cent of the total cultivated area, the production of these parcels of land represented in 1937 21 per cent of the overall production of the country, and the personal livestock of the peasants represented 55 per cent of the sheep and 40 per cent of the cattle. Finally, co-operative ownership imposed itself definitely during this period, since on the eve of the war the kolkhozes represented 116 million hectares while the State farms only covered 12 million hectares.

The peasants were then turned back upon themselves, on their memories and their bitterness – the devastated villages in which it was often impossible to start again fostered these grievances – and they formed an isolated element, unassimilable by Soviet society. Badly under-represented in the Party, the peasants were no longer part of political society but existed on its fringes. Thus, on the eve of the war, Soviet society showed new characteristics which had to be eradicated. More than twenty years after the Revolution, the disappearance of the antagonistic classes had not led to the formation of a coherent society, but to the perpetuation of three different groups, a privileged élite, and a working class and a peasantry which were not so privileged.

THE MORAL TRANSFORMATION OF SOCIETY

But more important even than the sociological transformation was the moral transformation of the Party and of the whole of the new élite described by Molotov, and which more and more formed the basis of Soviet society. This moral transformation sprang first from the fact that the intelligentsia, considered as the cream of the nation, had emerged unscathed from the crucible of the years 1934– 38 in which it had watched the disappearance of many of its own kind. The memory of the difficult years, the danger from which it had escaped, led the intelligentsia continually to try to consolidate both its moral and its material security. Here one comes to an extremely important ideological evolution, the legitimisation of material success, which was totally new in the communist psychology. To live better than the rest of the nation was no longer something to be condemned, but on the contrary it was desirable because a new link was established between material wealth – quite relative moreover – and socialist virtue, thus between wealth and security. The reasons for this evolution were obvious. In order to encourage the working class to work the authorities had increased the material incentives: productivity bonuses, exceptional rewards given to the stakhanovites, etc. The gap between the average worker and the 'hero of socialist labour' was widened and the difference was material and financial rather than moral. This led to an implicit conclusion which was that those who enjoyed a higher standard of living were precisely those who had worked hardest for communism, thus were the better communists. Whereas under Lenin, it had been impossible to show that one was enjoying a privileged standard of living, now from the 1930s on, the road to material advantages was also the road to being called a 'good communist', thus a means of survival in the strictest sense of the word.

The spirit of sacrifice and egalitarianism which had dominated Lenin's party had thus yielded to a desire for well-being and security which the regime had approved. The evolution of Soviet society in this direction had followed this course continuously since 1930 and in 1939 the doctrine of success, not only political and intellectual, but also social, was translated by material advantages and was one of the essential components of the new Soviet political culture.

But the legitimisation of success was only one of its aspects. Another concerning society as a whole was added to the one which concerned the privileged. During the 1930s, new social models were created and circulated by the literature and the media which were tightly controlled by the Party. These models showed what Soviet man should be and what were his relations with society and those in power. They also represented a complete break with the models which had prevailed immediately after the Revolution. The literature of the 1920s revealed very clearly the fundamental social values which the Revolution wanted to imprint upon the collective consciousness. It exalted the masses, the modest undistinguished citizens who made up the masses and shared the feeling of belonging to an egalitarian and fraternal society. Literature and art in general at that time tended to listen to the masses and to identify with them. Anonymous workers were promoted to the ranks of authors because their experience which embraced, it was thought, the whole society should serve as a model for all. When the writer or the artist was not eclipsed by the man from the rank and file, he put himself at his service and on his level. This society of the lowly was woven together by two strands: that of the social and moral coherence around a precise pole, the Party and its ideals; that of the building in common of a new world in which everyone's efforts were equally necessary. It was this model which was held up in the 1920s and which was gradually to disappear during the first Five-Year Plan. In the effort to change in which the USSR was engaged, there was no place for egalitarianism. What counted was the capacity of the individual to play a greater or smaller part in this change. It was his qualifications, his usefulness. Seen from this angle, men were far from equal and society tended to draw up a scale of values and consequently of individuals. Those who, because of their qualifications or an exceptional determination, were irreplaceable in the common effort, detached themselves from the masses. Knowledge, technical expertise were the supreme virtues. This change took place simultaneously in all spheres. The setting up of a scale of salaries adopted in 1931 had as a corollary the re-establishment of a social scale which appeared in the ideology. Writers were encouraged to concentrate on men who could really be an inspiration to society, that is, no longer on the crowd, on the lowly, but on those who were in the vanguard of the economic effort: the cadres and the experts. No one any longer believed that the experience of the anonymous workers had any importance in forging a new social consciousness. No one imagined, moreover, that the worker had himself to transmit this experience. The task of creating these models was confined to those who had the ability to do so, the ideologists, the professional writers. These 'engineers of minds' were given the task of presenting the masses with convincing models, transmitters of the social values that the Party deemed essential to the country's development.

Two models stood out in the sphere of labour relations. At the top were placed those who possessed the know-how and the technology and who were the heroes of Soviet society in the 1930s. They were the best, those who were indispensable to the general progress and who gave a lead to an ignorant mass, condemned without their help to inertia. But some individuals also emerged from that mass to make up, behind the glorious cohorts of the specialists, a second category of *positive heroes*. These were 'the best' among the masses, those who through an exceptional effort of will, an acute consciousness of the tasks which had to be accomplished pushed up through the ranks to become 'shock workers'. The embodiment of the lowly which *consciousness* had uprooted from the masses to individualise them, to give them their own place in the society was the Stakhanov worker, transformed by his exceptional production into a hero. With him a whole movement was forged, *stakhanovism*, which justified the emulation, the continuous rise in the norms of work and the growing demands of those in power on the productive capacity of the masses. Stakhanovism was a response to the lassitude of the people, an incitement to continuous effort, the sign that it was always possible to do the impossible. Stakhanovism was also a method of toning down the absolute inegalitarianism of the 1930s. What the example of Stakhanov tended to show was that in fact in a hierarchised society, knowledge was not the only road to social promotion; that everyone could, from his place, no matter how humble it might be, attain promotion, if he consciously made an effort to do so. The social model of the 1930s, while remaining strongly hierarchised, still made concessions to egalitarian aspirations. Stakhanov and his emulators were to be its guarantors. Literature was mobilised to impress upon the collective consciousness this new model of society, and it did so in a new style which also revealed the changes which had taken place. Although the literature of the 1920s was invited to use the ordinary language of daily use accessible to all, language which represented the daily values and heroes, the trend was reversed in the next decade. In order to praise the best the language of daily life was unsuitable. Epic terms were needed to describe the engineers or the 'shock workers' and these terms took over the language of the epics of pre-revolutionary history. Because the place of these heroes was exceptional, because it justified exceptional privileges, it was described in epic or fantastic terms. In following in the tradition of the *chansons de geste* or of the tales of the pre-revolutionary epoch, these works glorifying the transformation of the Soviet State had to take over the whole cultural realm to the detriment of a great part of the works of the past.

Thus the values conveyed by the old works disappeared to be replaced by the values honoured by Soviet society: organisation into a hierarchy of tasks and privileges, inequality, discipline and submission to those in authority. Because the form in which this new social culture was expressed was largely borrowed from the past, the gap was easy to bridge. After 1937, the works of the past were gradually incorporated into this new culture which was to add a regained national dimension to the social one. But the justified inegalitarianism and the stratification of society were also complemented at the beginning of the 1930s by another characteristic of the new political culture concerning the relations of men with the authorities, that is with the conception of authority. In the 1920s, in spite of the growth of the bureaucracy and of its excesses, the proposed social model was far from authoritarian; the society massed behind a collectivity, the Party, with which it identified itself. Here also, the change which took place at the beginning of the decade was considerable. The society in structuring itself organised itself this time on an authoritarian model, in which authority passed from a large and still impersonal entity which was the Party to the protective guardian figure of Stalin. In this society, in which burgeoning terror was to destroy all the traditional refuges and links of loyalty, relations were established directly between the individual and Stalin. This change was understandable because the crises within the Party had undermined its natural authority and left only one fixed point, Stalin, to whom the recantations and the self-criticisms of his adversaries had given almost supernatural authority. But also this change was conceived and speeded up by the development of social models which established this type of privileged relations. In this respect two social prototypes played a considerable role in the elaboration of the collective consciousness. One concerned childhood, the other the mass of the workers.

The best known hero presented to the children in the whole Stalinist period was Pavlik Morozov. This young pioneer, when he was thirteen, distinguished himself by denouncing his father to the police for taking part in a 'plot fomented by the kulaks'. For a generation of children and adolescents, Pavlik Morozov was the embodiment of a genuine Soviet conscience. He defined by his gesture a scale of social relations which the whole Stalinist epoch was to strengthen. The 'good' Soviet citizen was the one who was, above all, a member of the Soviet community, and only incidentally of the family group with which he could only identify himself if the group was in tune with the whole Soviet group. In rejecting his family and in denouncing his father, Pavlik Morozov was simply turning towards the group of which he was fundamentally a member. With the years, his story assumed a more definite content. More than towards the group, it was towards the Father of the group that he turned, towards Stalin. Compared with this social group, his natural father carried hardly any weight and his disappearance did not deprive Pavlik Morozov of his parent. Is it surprising that in the years of the purges his example was followed by countless children? The fear of sharing the fate of a father whom they had not denounced as a precaution lay doubtless at the root of innumerable denunciations; but the constantly presented influence of this example must not be underestimated for it had gradually placed the whole of society under Stalin's parental authority.

The same tendency to form a privileged dialogue between the man in power and the individual was to be found again in the stakhanovist model. When Alexis Stakhanov was invited to tell his compatriots how he had been able to achieve his exploit, he referred neither to the conditions in which he worked nor to a technical explanation, but described the inspiration he had received from a speech by Stalin on the radio, the evening before his exploit. Here again, it was Stalin's moral authority, the confidence established between the man at the bottom and the man at the top which suddenly enabled the humble worker to escape from his position and become a hero. In the story of Pavlik Morozov, and in that of Stakhanov, it was not a correct understanding of the ideology, it was not communist fervour which enabled the ordinary individual to transform himself into a hero. Their unique source of inspiration was Stalin and it was the awareness of a direct relation with him which guided the conduct of these two social prototypes. This privileged relation of the *Guide* to the individual was to be reinforced when, during the same period, the cohort of Soviet heroes was increased by the exceptional figures, those who were inimitable because of the exceptional quality of their exploits: aviators, explorers, but also scholars. These new heroes were no longer models, but signs of the Soviet Promethean project since all asserted in one way or another man's domination of nature. Inaccessible heroes, they had with Stalin the same kind of direct relationship as had the shock workers or the child informers and they had a privileged place in the new social hierarchy. Their example, even though it could not be imitated, taught many lessons. It showed that human effort could dominate and transform everything; it showed man's capacity to surpass himself when fidelity to the Guide was the source of his inspiration. In the ever-growing gallery of Soviet heroes, these newcomers helped to differentiate the society and to justify the differences and its inequalities. Finally, all these heroes were used to set up a new political system, the system which drained the Party of its authority in favour of Stalin alone. Stalin derived his personal authority above all from the crises in to which he plunged the Party and from the way he had manipulated it. But at the same time, he created a new political culture which placed him quite naturally at the summit of a society organised in a hierarchy of which he was clearly the Father. In the 1930s, Soviet political vocabulary did not as yet use this expression which the war was gradually to introduce. But even before the war, the nature of the social relations which were forming on the cultural models drawn up in the 1930s clearly gave priority to this parental relation in society.

THE RENAISSANCE OF THE FAMILY

If one searches for a common denominator in the moral trends of Soviet society, it appears that this denominator is individualism, the individual interest seen as the responsibility of each individual's efforts, which takes the place of the collective conscience which Lenin and his companions had tried to develop. The atomisation of society and the ultimate consequence of the purges contributed not a little to this evolution.

The growing individualism developed in the 1930s was, however, counterbalanced just before the war by another phenomenon which also marked the moral evolution of society: the rehabilitation of the values of the family.

After the Revolution, the family unit had exploded under the pressure of circumstances, but also from that of the apostles of individual freedom and of women's liberation like Alexandra Kollontay. It must also be remembered that Lenin, who held very traditional views on this subject, never encouraged this trend and that he was, on the contrary, very concerned about the results of this evolution, particularly for the children. However, at the same time, as they managed to destroy the solidarity of the family by the penal measures of 1934–36, the Soviet authorities began to implement a policy which was to restructure the family unit and consequently return to the family its moral justification. This was first clearly seen in the measures of 1936 which were part of the attempt to reverse the falling birth-rate, which was causing grave concern. It was in this perspective that in 1936 laws were passed to restrict the freedom to divorce (hitherto the divorce needed merely to be registered with the civil courts), to increase the financial and legal measures protecting maternity and, above all, to enforce a very restrictive policy on abortion which had hitherto been legal and completely free. This last reform was preceded by a very broad consultation of popular opinion. The problem was debated in all the factories and offices. Although, at the end of the day, the legislation adopted was to run counter to the unanimously expressed desire to maintain the former liberal ideas, it was nevertheless significant that the Party wanted to prepare and associate public opinion for and with this reassessment of social values. Also in line with this policy, a significant fact was the wide publicity given to Stalin's visit to his mother in Georgia in 1936. This visit was a return to his roots in two senses, since it honoured simultaneously the mother and the motherland; it was a recognition of motherhood as a social value as well as of the motherland as a political value.

Although this change made little impact at that time on the Russians, it was of great importance in the general context of the USSR. The greater part of the non-Russian peoples, those on the southern borders, Muslim or not, were generally attached to a patriarchal conception of society, and the destruction of the family order had helped to strengthen their critical attitude towards the regime, and had driven them back on their own system of values, in which the social values assumed a nationalist meaning and strengthened the nationalist links. After the rifts caused by the purges, this rebuilding of the family was reassuring and in the case of the non-Russian peoples it reintegrated them, at least at this level, within the Soviet community.

Thus, on the eve of the war, in its official ideology as well as in the moral evolution of its citizens, the USSR looked very different from the country of 1928. The Revolution had broken with the whole past and those who were leading it were constructing a new society. Lenin's successors had set their country economically on the way to this radical remaking of the structures of society; at the same time, after gradually breaking their people through the uninterrupted purges, they had now built a bridge with the past and inserted their experience into the history of the peoples they governed. Year I of the Revolution had been replaced by nearly 1,000 years and the Soviet people whom they were trying to create found support not only in the future, but in the past. The dread of war had done much to bring about this change; the war itself was to show how right the choice had been.

Chapter five
THE GREAT PATRIOTIC WAR

The Second World War, which in the USSR is called the Great
Patriotic War – that is the war in which for the first time the proletariat had to defend its reconquered motherland – is of considerable importance to the later history of the Soviet Union. The first
open clash of the socialist world with the world outside, coming
immediately after a particularly troubled period, the war was to
be a decisive test for the State and the Soviet nation in which their
cohesion and their capacity to survive were put to the test. The
progress of the war, and the political choices which it entailed were
to leave an enduring mark on the organisation of the State, the
aspirations of the people and the ideology, and the USSR in 1945
was to be greatly influenced by the solutions adopted during the
conflict.

THE MILITARY COLLAPSE OF THE USSR

At dawn, on 22 June 1941, more than 3 million German troops
invaded Soviet territory and for six months advanced by forced
marches in several directions. It was only at the beginning of December that they encountered any resistance. Von Rundstedt was
forced to abandon Rostov, while in front of Moscow the Red Army
on the 6th launched a counter-offensive. The cold, Russia's old ally
in times of invasion, set in at the same time and paralysed the
German army. On 7 December 1941, the Japanese attack on Pearl
Harbor put an end to the German hope that Japan, now at war
with the United States and Great Britain, would open a second
front in the Far East which would indeed have crippled the USSR.
Thus, by the end of 1941, Hitler's plan to finish off the USSR in a
few months had failed; new alliances were forged and slowly the
tide of fortune turned.

But it was a long time before this change made any impact on the USSR. At the end of 1941, the results of the first months of the war had been tragic; over 2 million Soviet soldiers had been taken prisoner, leaving in enemy hands nearly 18,000 tanks.

The part of Soviet territory occupied was important in land and even more in terms of the economy: 40 per cent of the Soviet population lived there; a large part of the industrial resources and potential – 65 per cent of the coal, 68 per cent of the iron, 60 per cent of the steel and aluminium, 40 per cent of the railway equipment; in the food sector, the situation was even worse, if this were possible; 84 per cent of the sugar supplies and 40 per cent of the cereal production were in the occupied zone.

The military collapse which had led to this unbelievable situation had been very rapid; the Red Army had been encircled without difficulty in various pockets and the bewildered population was at first unable either to resist or to think up any system of defence.

At first sight, this collapse was astonishing and Stalin, who realised this, mobilised a great many historians to explain and to justify it. During the war, Stalin laid the blame for the first early defeats on the inefficiency of the Soviet military leaders, but he finally opted for an explanation which was more favourable to the Soviet system: the element of the surprise attack. In the *Large Soviet Encyclopedia*, the article written in 1951 on the war explains that the USSR was prepared for this eventuality and that its military and industrial potential had been strengthened, as proved by the final outcome: but the suddenness of the German attack had taken the government by surprise. Nevertheless, one of the foundations of Soviet historiography of the war was to 'forget' the first six months and to emphasise the final victory.

It is clear that the Stalinist historians were right about the policy of the USSR before 1941 in the sphere of military affairs. After 1938, a great effort was made to provide the USSR with an efficient army in view of the coming conflict. The military budget had been increased sevenfold between 1934 and 1939, and the men under arms and the equipment had followed the same upward curve. In 1934, there were 900,000 serving men, in 1939 this figure had risen to 5 million and in 1941 to 6 million. At the time of the German invasion, the Soviet army was, from the numerical point of view, vastly superior to the German army engaged on Russian soil. Moreover, since 1939, Soviet industry had been geared towards the production of military equipment. The army had not only grown numerically, but a great effort had been made to provide it with a solid moral framework. In 1938, discipline had been re-established and the authority of the military leaders had become incontrovertible; it was strengthened again in 1940 by the re-establishment of a unified military command, which had been destroyed in 1937 during the campaign against Tukhachevsky. The political commissar who shared the authority of the commander-in-chief was replaced by a political commander, assistant to the military leader and, except for a period of hesitation between 1941 and 1942, this situation has prevailed ever since. Military authority, justified by the demands of efficiency, took precedence over political concerns. Seen from this point of view, any discussion of the military ranks established after the Revolution was, after 1940, tantamount to treason. The officer – whose position was strengthened by the ranks which had been restored to them – possessed real authority and enjoyed considerable prestige. What then was the explanation for the fact that this army which had been so strengthened, was so easily surrounded and put to flight? The explanation of the surprise factor invoked by Stalin is not supported by the historical documents. Warnings were not lacking from the armed forces, alarmed by the preparation in which they were taking part, as well as through diplomatic channels (on 13 April 1941 it was Churchill himself who sent a warning to Stalin of the imminence of the attack and the information was confirmed by a report from the spy Sorge giving the date). Besides, surprise is not enough to explain the extent of the reverses.

In 1956, Khrushchev, analysing the problem, found another explanation as simple as Stalin's; this was that Stalin's authoritarianism and lack of foresight had alone been responsible for the defeats. This comes very near to the truth, at least to one of its essential aspects. The leaders who had survived the purges were haunted by the fear of disagreeing with Stalin, and in so doing, of endangering themselves. In order to preserve their own security, they had abandoned all power into Stalin's hands: his authority was unquestioned. This had an adverse effect upon the preparations for war on which Stalin had been able to impose his own military ideas, which were extremely old-fashioned.

Stalin had in fact his own ideas about the art of war. Before 1937, he had clashed with the Soviet marshals, above all with Tukhachevsky, and once they had been liquidated he was able to impose his own ideas on the USSR. These centred around three ideas. First of all he was convinced that there would never be any fighting on Russian soil; the ineluctable deduction from this idea was that the USSR would never be attacked. The second certainty was that in any war it was necessary to be the 'aggressor' and not the one against whom the aggression was directed; therefore one must wage an offensive and not a defensive war. Stalin, convinced that he could strike first, had directed the whole Soviet military technique and the plan of action of the Soviet troops towards the prospect of an offensive war, without ever foreseeing the need to defend Russian soil. Finally, in the completely hypothetical case of an attack, it was clear to Stalin that this would be crushed immediately by an uprising of the Western proletariat who would never acquiesce in an attack on the homeland of socialism. This naïve confidence in the solidarity of the Western proletariat was astonishing in view of the fact that already in 1918 the infant Soviet State had been cruelly let down, and it is clear that Stalin's confidence was baseless. In spite of this somewhat unilateral view of a future war, Stalin's foreign policy was directed towards the idea that war was inevitable and he tried to avert and then to delay it. At first, he was eager to enlist the support of the Western democracies, but after Munich he concluded that an alliance with them would not be adequate protection and he then signed the Nazi Soviet Pact in 1939. This pact, regarded not as a lasting alliance, but as a means by which German ambitions could be temporarily deflected from the USSR was however – the documents prove it – taken very seriously by Stalin who cherished the astonishing illusion that Hitler would respect it. Stalin was apparently convinced that the USSR in 1941 could not withstand the shock of a war and he hoped to delay Hitler until 1942 when he himself thought that he could take the initiative. The only eventuality which he apparently excluded was that Hitler would not be inclined to wait until the USSR was ready to resist him. Thus, until 22 June 1941, Stalin constantly rejected the early warnings, which came to him from all quarters regarding them as essentially British provocations which were designed to make him open a second front, thus easing the British war effort. This was how he interpreted the Rudolf Hess affair; Hess arrived in Britain in May 1941 and warned the British government that an attack on the USSR was imminent, suggesting that the Russians and the Germans should be left to fight it out. Even the warning of such an exceptional source left Stalin indifferent and convinced once more that it was a provocation. To his own military leaders who warned him of the disquieting movements of German troops and of planes flying over Soviet territory, he always gave the same reply: 'We must not yield either to German provocation or to blackmail.'

Here, it seems, lies Stalin's main responsibility; he completely ignored the way the war was developing and Hitler's war aims, and constantly underestimated Hitler's determination to turn the USSR and its riches into a German dependency.

There are many examples of Stalin's blindness. After 15 May 1941, the Soviet military leaders, concerned by the rapid deterioration in German-Soviet relations, made preparations for the German attack which they kept secret from the government. They moved troops to defensive positions. Thus, in June, Konyev's army was moved from the north of the Caucasus to the Ukraine and on 10 June the units of the military region of Kiev began to occupy the unfinished fortified lines along the frontier. Hearing of this last measure, Moscow sent an imperative countermand to 'cancel immediately and inform us of the name of the man who gave this unauthorised order'. Thus, many times, the troops were brought back to their former positions allowing the German army to encircle them with ease. On 14 June 1941, while the world press was full of the coming conflict, the Soviet newspapers published a communiqúe from Tass which acknowledged the existence of German troop movements on the frontiers of the USSR and stated that these movements had no bearing upon the future of the Nazi-Soviet Pact, that the USSR believed that they were perfectly legitimate manoeuvres and remained convinced of Germany's loyalty towards the USSR. The communiqué, which once again harped on the theme of a provocation, had a considerable impact on the USSR, and resulted in a slowing down of the mobilisation. During the first fortnight in June, the Soviet people had become increasingly concerned and a sort of spontaneous mobilisation had begun: leave was almost entirely suspended, the officers staying with their units, the army preparing for the attack. After 14 June, the government encouraged growing optimism among the people which was an extraordinary contrast to the tension in the rest of the world. On 19 June, an editorial in *Pravda* was devoted to the 'workers' summer break', and the reporter of the *New York Times* was astounded by the fact that the Moscow population was more interested in football matches than in the approaching conflict. The 22nd was equally calm, as *Pravda* was concerned with Lermontov's centenary and devoted its editorial to 'the people's interest in his school'.

When, around three o'clock in the morning, the German divisions crossed the western frontier of the USSR, the Soviet leaders were in total disarray. No one dared to reply to the military leaders in the frontier regions which had already been attacked and who were asking for orders and it was not until seven o'clock in the morning, three hours after the attack, that the People's Commissar for Defence at last gave the first very restricted order, since the Soviet Air Force was not authorised to strike over a distance of more than 100 to 150 km. The argument that this was a provocation still persisted. During the decisive hours, contradictory orders and delaying tactics helped to increase the confusion. It was only in the evening of 22 June, when 100 aerodromes and more than 1,000 Soviet planes had been destroyed, when the German army had crossed the Neman, besieged Brest-Litovsk and marched on Lvov that the Defence Commissar ordered the Soviet army to take the offensive. Thus, even after the attack, Stalin hesitated, refusing to act immediately and clung to his theory of an offensive war.

There were also two other serious causes of weakness: an often arbitrary policy on equipment and the disorganisation of the officer corps by the purges.

The Soviet war industry had been developed after 1938–39; but here again Stalin's continual intervention in the choice of military equipment had often been disastrous. The memoirs of the military leaders give some very amusing details about this intervention, as for instance the confusion made by Stalin between the model of gun used in 1914 and in 1940, when it was necessary to choose the model best adapted to the needs of modern warfare. Similarly, he ordered the fortifications along the 1939 frontier to be dismantled in order to build new ones along the new frontier, forgetting that several years were needed for this and that in the meantime the USSR would remain without any protective fortifications in the west.

The military collapse was to give rise to a grave economic problem: this was how could Soviet industry be protected. In fact, after the first weeks of the war, most of the economic potential of the USSR was threatened by destruction was under the threat of being destroyed or of falling into German hands. We have seen above the importance to the economy of the country of the resources in the area in which the Germans were advancing; a few figures will show the extent of the disaster. The area contained 31,850 large enterprises – metallurgy, mechanical engineering, agricultural equipment, the chemical and food processing industries, etc.; 1,135 mines, 61 power-stations, 65,000 km of railway, 98,000 kolkhozes, 1,876 sovkhozes, 2,890 MTS and 88 million inhabitants.

In spite of its disarray, the Soviet government began, forty-eight hours after the invasion, to take measures to protect the threatened equipment. On 24 June 1941, an Evacuation Committee was created, under the presidency of L. Kaganovich assisted by A. Kosygin, N. Shvernik, B. Shaposhnikov, P. Popkov, N. Dubrovin, S. L. Kruglov and A. Kirpichnikov. On 26 June Mikoyan became a member of this committee as vice-president and on 1 July, he was replaced by Pervukhin. On 16 July, the Defence Committee which had been created a few days before placed the Committee for Evacuation under the presidency of N. Shvernik, assisted in August by General Zakharov. On 26 September, a Department for the Evacuation of the Population was created within the Evacuation Committee and chaired by the President of the Sovnarkom of the RSFSR, K. D. Pamfilov. This department existed until 31 January 1944. Finally on 25 October, a committee for the evacuation of the industrial and food resources of the regions close to the front completed these arrangements. One of the great difficulties facing the authorities whose task it was to carry out the evacuation was the inadequacy of the means of transport. From the beginning of the evacuation to 20 November 1941, 914,380 wagons were loaded with materials or persons. The distribution of the available wagons between the different priorities gave rise to many problems because they were in short supply; thus, for the evacuation of the metallurgical enterprises of the Donbass there were only 3,460 wagons instead of the 13,000 needed. The same was true of the river transport where the authorities had to deal with another problem, that of the cold which very soon made the rivers impassable. Because of these difficulties, the evacuation was often delayed at the start or along the way. In December 1941 many transports were held up in the transit centres, and a new body was set up to deal with this, to organise the discharge of the material at fixed points and to direct it towards its final destination. In this body, created on 25 December 1941, N. Voznesensky played an important part.

The Central Committee and the Sovnarkom of the USSR in a common directive of 27 June 1941 defined the duties of the different bodies as 'the evacuation and resettlement of men and materials'.

The evacuation of the industrial potential took place in two seasons: the summer and autumn of 1941 and the summer and autumn of 1942.